LEABHARLANNA CHONTAE FHINE GALL
FINGAL COUNTY LIBRARIES

Items should be returned on or before the last date shown below. Items may be renewed by personal application, writing, telephone or by accessing the online Catalogue Service on Fingal Libraries' website. To renew give date due, borrower ticket number and PIN number if using online catalogue. Fines are charged on overdue items and will include postage incurred in recovery. Damage to, or loss of items will be charged to the borrower

Date Due	Date Due	Date Due

More Tales Behind the Tombstones

More Deaths and Burials of the Old West's Most Nefarious Outlaws, Notorious Women, and Celebrated Lawmen

Chris Enss

TWODOT®

GUILFORD, CONNECTICUT
HELENA, MONTANA

A · TWODOT® · BOOK

An imprint of Rowman & Littlefield
TwoDot is a registered trademark of Rowman & Littlefield.

Distributed by NATIONAL BOOK NETWORK

Copyright © 2015 by Chris Enss
Text design: Lisa Reneson

British Library Cataloguing in Publication Information Available

Library of Congress Cataloging-in-Publication Data

ISBN 978-0-7627-9630-4 (paperback)
ISBN 978-1-4930-1788-1 (e-book)

♾™ The paper used in this publication meets the minimum requirements of American National Standard for Information Sciences—Permanence of Paper for Printed Library Materials, ANSI/NISO Z39.48-1992.

Contents

CONTENTS

Acknowledgments

A book of this sort is never a solitary venture. It all comes together through the combined efforts of those in historical societies, archives departments, libraries, and museums. I owe a debt of gratitude to the following organizations and individuals who helped to bring this project about:

The Nevada County Historical Society
The California State Library
The Herbert Hoover Presidential Library-Museum
Wyoming State Archives
Denver Public Library
Vassar College Libraries
South Dakota State Historical Society
Deadwood History, Inc.
Idaho State Archives
Nancy Sherbert at the Kansas State Historical Society
Michael Diaz at the Whitehead Memorial Museum
Warren Hunting Smith Library in Geneva, New York
Terry Zinn at the Oklahoma Historical Society
Glen Gambill at the Lamar County Historical Museum
Debby Craigo at the Allegheny Cemetery in Pittsburgh, Pennsylvania
And most especially, Terry Ommen, Tulare County, California Historian

As always, thanks to my editor, Erin Turner, for her continued belief in my writing. I'm grateful to be able to work for her.

Introduction

Visitors walking through the graveyards often times find themselves stepping over weeds that have grown around fallen headstones. Sadly, the final resting place for many small families and communities has been left unattended or even forgotten. The seasons have taken with them the names chiseled in the granite, nearly erasing all memory of those mourned beneath the dilapidated tombstones.

Aside from the normal life and death cycle in New England, it is estimated that one in every seventeen people died on the journey west from 1847 to 1900. Oftentimes the men, women, and children who died en route to the gold hills of California and Colorado, or the fertile farmlands of the Pacific Northwest, were buried on the spot where they died. A proper burial and lengthy funeral were forfeited in favor of pushing on to the far-off destination. Traveling across the plains demanded that sojourners be constantly on the move. The threat of bad weather, hostile Indians, wild animals, or desperados kept pioneers from staying too long in one area.

Contrary to popular belief, the thousands of settlers who perished on the trail west did not solely die in gunfights or Indian attacks. Scorching deserts, starvation, and dehydration claimed many lives. Poor sanitation bred typhoid, cholera, and pneumonia. Blood poisoning brought on by a cut or scrape from a sharp object, or shock from an accident, such as a wagon spilling over with travelers inside, brought about numerous deaths as well.

There were pioneers, though, who could not be persuaded to forgo a ceremonial funeral if they lost a loved one. Nothing could keep them from burying the deceased in a plot where they could be remembered. A section of ground in a scenic location with trees to shade the grave was the preferred spot. To leave someone dear in an unmarked plot was impossible for some to accept.

As pioneers established homesteads and built towns around their farms and ranches, the dead were buried either in family cemeteries near where they had lived or next to churches where they worshipped. For nineteenth-century ancestors, it was important to remember death. The fact of death served as a reminder to those who continued on to persevere and do good works as preparation for a final judgment by a righteous God.

Whatever the cause of death or wherever it occurred, the need to take care of a deceased person's remains was a necessity. Until the discovery of formaldehyde in 1867, and the subsequent introduction of the product and its use as an acceptable embalming method in America in 1872, there were limited ways to deal with the dead. Immediate burial was preferred. If a person died in the winter and the ground was frozen and a grave could not be dug, the body was stored in a barn or woodshed until the earth thawed and the departed could be buried.

As in the cities, carpenters in mining camps or cattle towns were usually the undertakers, since they had the tools and supplies to build coffins. The wooden caskets might be lined with white linen if it was supplied by the deceased's family or friends. Sextons, people who looked after a church and churchyard, would determine where in the cemetery a person was to be buried. They would also dig the grave and fill it again.

People who lived in small towns would often gather at the graveyard where the coffin was placed atop two sawhorses. For those who lived in less rural areas, there were hearses to rent to transport the dead from the undertaker's office to the cemetery. The vehicle had glass sides and was decorated with elaborate carvings and brass ornaments. On top were tall, shako-like plumes, one on each corner.

While cemeteries house the dead, the tombstones record not only their pleasures, sorrows, and hopes for an afterlife, but also more than they realize of their history, ethnicity, and culture. In this book are true stories about thirty real people who are buried in marked and unmarked graves throughout the frontier and elsewhere. How these famous and infamous individuals lived and then exited this world is reflected on their headstones. Tales of their demise add details of their courage, adventure, hardship, and joy not included on those tombstones.

The dead herein will never exhaust their potential to enlighten.

Judge Roy Bean

d. 1903

I aim to shoot the hell out of anybody that tries to stop me. I aim to mind my own business, and aim to back up the law.

—JUDGE ROY BEAN

With the passing of Judge Roy Bean, who referred to himself as the "Law West of the Pecos," the rowdy frontier lost one of its most unusual and picturesque characters. It was Judge Bean who was said to have held an inquest on the body of an unknown man found in his precinct and, finding on the corpse a pistol and $40 in cash, proclaimed the dead man guilty of carrying a concealed weapon and fined him $40, which was forthwith collected from the pocket of the offender.

There were no customers from Judge Roy Bean's opera house and saloon by his side when he died on March 16, 1903; no friends from the Langtry, Texas, community where he had resided; no lawbreakers to be tried and sentenced. Judge Bean's son, Sam, was the only one with him when he passed.

The stout, seventy-eight-year-old man with a gray beard spent his last hours on earth in a near comatose state unaware of

Judge Roy Bean Saloon and Justice Court LIBRARY OF CONGRESS HABS TEX,233-LANG,1--1

where he was or who he was. He died of heart and lung complications exacerbated by alcohol.

Roy was born in a cabin in Mason County, Kentucky, in 1823, but he spent his childhood in Independence, Missouri. He followed his older brother to the Southwest in 1846, and the pair opened a trading post in Chihuahua, Mexico.

In 1848, eighteen-year-old Roy killed a desperado trying to steal from him and fled the area to escape arrest. There were several more run-ins with the law between 1849 and 1862. In 1862, Roy decided to join the army to fight for the North in the Civil War. He married Virginia Chavez in 1866 and the couple settled in San Antonio, Texas. Roy and his wife had four children, but the marriage was rocky and didn't last.

When the Southern Pacific Railroad began its extension from San Antonio to the Rio Grande, Roy followed the line with a movable house that featured a saloon. During one of the rides he met an attorney from Chicago who regaled him with stories of how the justice system worked in the eastern states. The fascinating details of law and order stuck with Roy, and when he was appointed justice of the peace at a railroad stop in West Texas he decided to employ all he had learned from the Chicagoan.

Roy Bean gave the temporary railroad stop that grew into a town its name. He called the spot Vinegaroon. A vinegaroon is a whip-tailed scorpion common in that region. The name was appropriate as well as symbolic. "I aim to run a square place," the judge informed all potential customers. "I aim to shoot the hell out of anybody that tries to stop me. I aim to mind my own business, and aim to back up the law."

"What law?" some brave railroad worker ventured to ask. "There hasn't been any sign of civilized law this far west yet."

"My own!" Judge Bean roared. "I'm the law from now on. I'm the law west of the Pecos."

Judge Roy Bean hung a sign in front of his establishment that read, "Roy Bean, Notary Public, Ice Cold Beer. Judge Roy Bean, Law West of the Pecos." The railroad executives liked it. It was convenient and gave the railroad a location to tie itself to, and somebody to punish thieves and other rowdy cowboys. Cattle ranchers came in fast, and they liked the semblance of law, too. They had no time to organize and hold elections, so they took Roy Bean on as the authority.

Roy's actions as a judge were quite eccentric. He called court to order with the butt of a six-gun, officiated at any occasion for a price, and ruled on inquests.

The town of Vinegaroon slowly died out, but Judge Roy Bean's position as justice of the peace remained intact. He and the job simply moved on with the Southern Pacific Railroad to an area southwest of the former Vinegaroon. "He [Judge Bean] had not been a justice a month in Langtry before he distinguished himself with a historic ruling," a report in the April 15, 1904, edition of the Scandia, Kansas, newspaper, the *Scandia Journal,* read. The matter involved the marriage and divorce of two Hispanic couples, and the judge's decision attracted attention from a higher court.

Couples came from miles in every direction to have the notorious judge marry them. Among those who came were two Hispanic couples. The judge married them. Two months later they appeared before him again. They had made a mistake, they said, and wanted to swap wives. "That's easy," said the judge, "I'll divorce you."

He gave the necessary decision in open court and collected $15 from each of the men. The Hispanic couples then changed wives and started home satisfied. They did not get far when the judge ordered them back to court. "You must be married again," he said. "Five dollars apiece, please."

The couples protested, but the judge insisted that he could not let them go back unmarried, for it was against the law. The case was brought to the attention of a higher court judge, who wrote, "It's all right this time, but please don't divorce anymore couples." Judge Roy Bean agreed, but continued doing just as he pleased.

Judge Bean was infatuated with stage actress Lillie Langtry and plastered the interior of his saloon and courtroom with photographs of her from magazines and newspapers. He renamed his business The Jersey Lilly in her honor and renamed the town Langtry.

According to the October 20, 1910, edition of the *Oakland Tribune,* Judge Bean wrote a letter a day to Lillie Langtry. He'd spend an hour or more on each letter, during which time all business in his establishment would be at a polite standstill. Lillie never responded.

The judge eventually traveled to see the famous beauty perform. He never spoke to her and never tried to go backstage. He was content only to watch her glide about from one side of the stage to another. He continued to write to her until he died.

On March 15, 1903, Judge Roy Bean made a trip to San Antonio, Texas, to attend a cockfight. He drank until he passed out and had to be escorted back to his home in Langtry. He never recovered.

In late 1903, Lillie Langtry decided to visit her famous fan. She toured his Jersey Lilly saloon and drank a toast in his honor. Langtry residents gave her Judge Bean's pet bear, which had been chained for years to the foot of his bed. The animal ran off as soon as it was released. Lillie was then presented with the judge's revolvers.

Judge Roy Bean was laid to rest in Del Rio, Texas. His tombstone reads "Judge Roy Bean, Justice of the Peace, Law West of the Pecos."

Judge Roy Bean's grave marker WHITEHEAD MEMORIAL MUSEUM, DEL RIO, TEXAS

James Beckwourth

d. 1866

*His courage is of the highest order, and probably no man
ever lived who has met with more personal adventure
involving danger to life, though in this respect he is not
an exception to all mountaineers and hunters who early
engaged in the fur trade and faced the perils of an unknown wilderness.*

—PREFACE (WRITTEN BY THOMAS D. BONNER)
TO *THE LIFE AND ADVENTURES OF JAMES P. BECKWOURTH*

James Beckwourth was one of the most legendary mountain men
of the early 1800s. He was the son of a Maryland Irishman and a
slave girl, and he was born in Virginia in 1798. When he was very
young, his family moved to St. Charles, Missouri. James worked as
an apprentice to a blacksmith until the age of nineteen, when he
left the anvil and the forge to sign on as a trapper with the Missouri
Fur Company, then challenging Hudson Bay trappers working the
rich beaver streams beyond the crest of the Rockies.

In 1824, Beckwourth joined William H. Ashley and Andrew
Henry on a fur-trapping expedition in the Rocky Mountains; he
was one of the first trappers to go into the new country. During

James Beckwourth COURTESY WYOMING STATE ARCHIVES, DEPARTMENT OF STATE
PARKS & CULTURAL RESOURCES

various expeditions, he participated in skirmishes with the Blackfeet
and other Indians. He became skilled in the use of the bowie knife,
tomahawk, and gun.

In 1828, he was adopted into the Crow Indian tribe. He
packed his traps and buckskin shirts on his horses and moved to
the headwaters of the Powder Rivers and into a new life among
the ancient people. He proved himself quickly among his adopted

people and rose to the position of war chief. His skill as part of a raiding party to steal Comanche horses was masterful. His prowess and bravery in battle against the hated Blackfoot Indians earned him the name Bloody Arm.

James Beckwourth helped make the Crow a more powerful nation. No more would they give away a tanned buffalo hide for a pint of trade whiskey. Bloody Arm knew the value of hides and the wiles of the whites. He knew the worth of powder and ball and traps and horses and finery for Crow women.

When a fur company opened a trading post among the feared Blackfeet, Beckwourth got the same company to make him its agent among the Crow to see that his adopted people were treated fairly in the trade of pelts for guns. When the beaver trade began fading, Beckwourth went to the Southwest and joined with another ex–mountain man to lead a war party of Utes to raid Spanish ranches in Southern California. They headed east with three thousand head of California horses.

He spent a while in Taos, moved onto Colorado to become a contract hunter supplying meat in places like Bent's Fort, and then became a trader among Indians. Showing up again in Southern California, he raised a company of Yanquix to fight Governor Micheltorena of Mexico in a quickie revolution.

By the time of the California Gold Rush and the westward movement of hundreds of wagon trains over the worst passes of the Sierra, James, then in his fifties, led a wagon train over a sizable mountain pass that was to be named after him. He still had years of adventure before him. He scouted for the Third Colorado Cavalry tracking Black Kettle to Sand Creek and turned away in disgust at the massacre.

At the age of sixty-eight, Beckwourth embarked on another venture, this one in a bid for peace. The Oglala Sioux were pressing the Crow to join against the whites. The US Army sent for Beckwourth to advise his adopted tribe. He thwarted the alliance.

Mystery surrounds James Beckwourth's death in Colorado in 1866 in a Crow village. Some historians note he was poisoned by a Crow warrior who caught him cavorting with his wife. The most reliable account of his passing reports that he was poisoned by order of the Crow's tribal council because he would not accept their offer to go on the warpath with them again. If they could not keep him as a chief, they decided to have the honor of burying him in their burial ground near Laramie, Wyoming. Beckwourth was seventy-eight when he died.

Chalk Beeson

d. 1912

He came to Dodge City when every man carried a gun, and the fittest survived. Beeson survived. But he is not fierce. He has not shot a man in several days.

—DODGE CITY, KANSAS, NEWSPAPER

Well-known Dodge City, Kansas, lawman and politician Chalk Beeson claimed he "drank bullets in his coffee for breakfast." Few doubted how tough Sheriff Beeson was—particularly desperados raising hell in Ford County, Kansas.

Born in Salem, Ohio, in 1876, the highly esteemed man had a reputation for tracking even the most wanted criminals until they were caught. In November 1892, Chalk decided to ride into the Oklahoma Territory on his own to capture the notorious Doolin Gang. The gang had robbed the Spearville Ford County Bank in broad daylight and Chalk was not going to let them get away with it.

According to the August 12, 1912, edition of the Hutchinson, Kansas, newspaper the *Hutchinson News*, Chalk was so provoked by the Doolin Gang's actions that he refused to wait until a posse was formed before he took out after the bandits. "He went to Oklahoma under an alias," the newspaper article read, "and when

Chalk Beeson KANSAS STATE HISTORICAL SOCIETY

he found the headquarters of the gang near Ingalls, he went to Guthrie and was appointed a deputy United States marshal, as he was far out of his jurisdiction as sheriff."

One particular man in the gang Chalk was determined to arrest was Oliver Yantes, who was living with a woman in a cabin five miles from Ingalls. Chalk and a lawman he believed he could trust rode to the Yantes cabin and they hid along the path a few feet away from the entrance. Chalk concluded that Yantes would have to travel the path the following morning in order to take care of his horses.

When Yantes appeared, Chalk ordered him to throw up his hands, but instead of doing what the officer ordered, the bandit attempted to run. The plan had been for the deputy to shoot the desperado if he offered resistance while Chalk watched in case other members of the gang were there. The mist had dampened the caps of the deputy's gun and when he failed to fire Chalk believed the lawman had been betrayed. Chalk fired on Yantes just as the woman ran from the house with the bandit's revolver. Yantes was fatally wounded and died before Chalk could get him to Ingalls.

Chalk collected the reward offered by the state, the banks, the railroads, and the insurance company for the apprehension of any member of the Doolin Gang, dead or alive.

In addition to serving three terms as sheriff of Ford County, Chalk also served as a representative of the area in the state legislature from 1902 to 1906. Chalk's abilities extended beyond his work in law enforcement and politics. He was an accomplished horse trainer and an expert musician. He could play the violin, trombone, and French horn. In 1885 Chalk founded the Dodge City Cowboy Band. The band was made up of more than eighteen men who played brass, percussion, and strings. The Dodge City Cowboy Band performed at the Long Branch Saloon, owned by Chalk, and entertained local citizenry by marching in parades. The band wore their best cowboy attire, including their six guns, which they fired in the air to punctuate a chord or musical phrase.

The tough and talented Chalk met his demise August 8, 1912. Three days prior to his death, Chalk was sitting atop his horse at the C.O.D. Ranch, watching a nearby road construction crew work. His mount was suddenly spooked. The horse bucked and reared and before Chalk was able to get the animal under control it threw him hard against the saddle horn. Chalk never recovered from the serious injury.

Chalk Beeson's well-attended funeral was held August 11, 1912, at his ranch. Local businessmen and luminaries spoke highly of the contributions he had made to the community. Benevolent and fraternal society members, as well as civic and church representatives, turned out to brag about all he had done to make Dodge City a safe place to live. Mourners reflected on Chalk's fine character and the positions of responsibility and trust he held in Ford County. One of Chalk's friends at the funeral admitted that the community believed that "just one of Chalk Beeson's strengths [was that he] could withstand the worst kind of injury."

Chalk Beeson's tombstone COURTESY OF BRENT HARRIS

Elizabeth Blackwell

d. 1910

*A lady, on his invitation, entered, whom he formally in-
troduced as Miss Elizabeth Blackwell. A hush fell upon the
class as if each member had been stricken with paralysis. A
death-like stillness prevailed during the lecture, and only
the newly arrived student took notes.*

—1911 RECOLLECTION BY A FORMER CLASSMATE OF ELIZABETH BLACKWELL

On Wednesday, January 25, 1911, physicians across the world
gathered at the great hall at the Academy of Medicine in New York
to honor America's first woman doctor, Elizabeth Blackwell. The
tenacious pioneer in the fight for the right of women to study and
practice medicine had died nine months prior to the event hon-
oring the contributions she made to the field. The audience was
composed largely of women, all of whom owed a debt of gratitude
to Elizabeth Blackwell.

Born in Bristol, England, on February 3, 1821, Elizabeth
immigrated to America in 1832 with her parents. Her desire to
attend school and study medicine began at an early age. Elizabeth
was twenty-six years old when she was admitted to New York's
Geneva College in 1847. She had applied to twenty institutions

before being accepted as a medical student at the prestigious university. The male students there believed Elizabeth's request was a joke and agreed to let her attend the classes based on that idea, but the daring young woman was not playing around. She prevailed and triumphed over taunts and bias while at school to earn her degree only two years after enrolling.

While in her last year of school, she treated an infant with an eye infection. As she was washing the baby's eye with water, she accidentally splattered the con-

Elizabeth Blackwell LIBRARY OF CONGRESS LC_USZ62-57850

taminated liquid in her own eye. Six months later she had the eye removed and replaced with a glass eye. Hospitals and dispensaries refused to admit her to practice at their facilities because of her partial blindness, and she was denounced by the press and from the pulpit because she was a woman who dared to practice medicine.

After graduating in 1849, Elizabeth found herself socially and professionally boycotted. Public sentiment was so against her for pursuing a career in a field deemed unladylike that she could not find a place to live anywhere in New York. Using funds given to her by her family, she built her own home in New York City.

In 1854, she borrowed the capital needed to build a small dispensary for women in the country. Most of the patients she worked with were poor. Patients were charged a mere $4 a week for services that would cost them $2,000 at another facility. Elizabeth also founded the Women's Medical College of New York, and, when the Civil War broke out, she assisted in launching the Sanitary Aid Association to promote hygiene and to campaign

Elizabeth Blackwell's tombstone HOBART AND WILLIAM SMITH COLLEGES ARCHIVES
AND SPECIAL COLLECTIONS

for better preventive medicine. In addition to maintaining her practice and creating benevolent community services, Elizabeth wrote a number of books on the subject of medicine. Two of her most popular titles were *Pioneer Work in Opening the Medical Profession for Women* and *Essays in Medical Sociology*.

By the turn of the century, Elizabeth Blackwell had retired from medicine and returned to England. In the spring of 1907, she was injured in a fall from which she never fully recovered. She died on May 31, 1910, from a stroke. The epitaph below the Celtic cross which marks her grave at Kilmun Churchyard on the Holy Loch, near Clyde, includes these words: "The first woman in modern times to graduate in medicine (1849) and the first to be placed on the British Medical Register (1859)." Elizabeth's courage and determination led the way for many other women to enter the field of medicine, and several of those women traveled west to work in their chosen profession and bring healing to the frontier.

Sister Blandina

d. 1941

*No work was foreign to her, provided it was God's work.
One knows not which to admire more, her instant grasp
of a difficult situation, or the coolness and resourcefulness
with which she met it.*

—PREFACE TO *AT THE END OF THE SANTA FE TRAIL*,
THE AUTOBIOGRAPHY OF SISTER BLANDINA SEGALE

With the influx of people to the Old West, towns sprang into existence, churches were formed, laws were enacted, and schools were established. Schools were considered necessary among the growing population, and good teachers along with them; without them, the children of the settlers would become the orphans of progress.

Among the populations pushing beyond the boundaries of the Mississippi River were daring female educators who hoped to find work teaching frontier boys and girls how to read and write. All that was initially required of teachers was that they be able to count, read, write, and mend a pen. However, these new schoolmarms were energetic, and they arrived able to do immeasurably more than the basics. Rosa Marie Segale was one such teacher.

Born on January 23, 1850, in Cicagna, Italy, Rosa came to America with her parents and three other siblings when she was four years old. The family settled in Cincinnati, where several of their other countrymen had made their home. Rosa had a difficult time in Ohio. Not being able to speak the language was a barrier, and, apart from her older sisters, she had no one to play with or talk to. It wasn't until her parents arranged for their children to receive English lessons that the young girl came into her own.

After attending finishing school and completing several music and Spanish language courses, Rosa entered a convent. Once she had taken her final vows, she was given the name Sister Blandina. A brief stint teaching in Dayton and Steubenville, Ohio, opened the door to her first westward assignment as a teacher in Trinidad, Colorado. From Colorado she went on to New Mexico. During her time in both locations, she kept a diary of her experiences. It was published in 1932 under the title *At the End of the Santa Fe Trail*.

During the time she lived in the West, Sister Blandina had many encounters with vigilantes and outlaws. She was never afraid to chastise those who took the law into their own hands or to care for wounded criminals. She had a knack for nursing and in the late 1870s not only helped raise funds to build hospitals for Indians, miners, and orphans, but also gave aid to a member of Billy the Kid's gang named Happy Jack. Billy wanted to kill the four doctors who refused to help his friend before they came to Sister Blandina, but she managed to talk him out of it. She looked after Happy Jack for nine months before he died.

Billy remembered Sister Blandina's act of kindness and in the spring of 1877 found a way to repay her. On a trip to Santa Fe from Trinidad, Billy the Kid refrained from robbing a stage the sister was on after recognizing she was on board.

Sister Blandina's time teaching in Santa Fe was rewarding, and she took on more than just educating the class on the basics—

Sister Blandina Segale COURTESY OF PALACE OF THE GOVERNORS (MNM/DCA) 067735

she was also a music instructor. Using a donated piano and organ, the sister taught students to read music and prepared them for end-of-year programs.

In August 1881, Sister Blandina was directed by the church to move to Albuquerque. Over the ten-year period she lived there, she helped build three schools, including a school for Indians, and a mission. She saw the Wild West evolve from an untamed frontier to a civilized country, and she anticipated even greater changes as time went on. As she shared in her memoirs:

> *What was sand-banks and adobe houses has been transformed into green fields and stone buildings. The transition period will cause many to forget the end of man's creation. When the sane period comes, there will be a further clearing up of mad house activities. The conscientious and level headed will emerge serene. The dishonest will fear exposure, the unsophisticated will be submerged, and the Catholic missionary apprehensive and on the alert to prevent wolves in sheep's clothing from entering the flock.*

On August 11, 1889, the Catholic Church recalled Sister Blandina to Trinidad. In 1897, she returned to the motherhouse in Cincinnati and worked with children, teaching and assisting attorneys in juvenile court cases. She also worked with Italian immigrant children and helped establish the Italian Welfare Center, which helped house the homeless and provide all in need with food and clothing.

In the winter of 1941, Sister Blandina was hospitalized with complications stemming from a broken hip. She died on February 23, 1941, a month after celebrating her ninety-first birthday. Many of her former students attended her funeral and remembered the purpose she lived by, which was "to teach and meet emergencies" as she saw fit. Sister Blandina is buried at the Sisters of Charity Cemetery in Cincinnati, Ohio.

Nellie Bly

d. 1922

Energy rightly applied and directed will accomplish anything.

—Nellie Bly's motto

On a summer day in the early 1880s an article called "What Girls Are Good For" appeared in the *Pittsburg Dispatch*. It took a firm stand against the new fad of hiring women to work in offices and shops. "A respectable woman," the article noted with authority, "remained at home until she married." If a husband eluded her, she had two choices left. She might go into teaching or into nursing, provided money for her training could be wangled from a reluctant father. Otherwise, she stayed under his roof or that of a relative and for the remainder of her life accepted the status of house worker or child's nurse, without pay.

The article expressed the customary male sentiments of the day more emphatically than usual because the editors were stirred up over the inroads being made by suffragettes. Radical females like Susan B. Anthony, openly militant in regard to votes for females, and Elizabeth Cady Stanton, champion of women's rights, went striding up and down the country with a following of "bloomer girls." Nobody knew better than the *Dispatch*'s managing editor, George A. Madden, that since the Civil War the manpower shortage had increasingly drawn women into mills and factories, but he felt a barricade must be erected against such an alarming trend. Women in politics were unthinkable, as obviously out of place there as they would be in such a masculine stronghold as his own, a newspaper office.

The article received the expected male commendation from Mr. Madden's business associates. He was happily married and his wife, busy with children, made no comment. Other

Nellie Bly LIBRARY OF CONGRESS LC_USZ62-59923

matters had taken its place in his active editorial mind when a few days later his memory was refreshed. Going through the morning mail, he read a letter and winced. Then he read it again, and a third time, even though it bore no signature, and for a reason. It was a reply to the "What Girls Are Good For" story, and it sizzled. It was a rebuke to the newspaper's old fashioned attitude, a declaration of independence for women, and a war cry to them to take their proper place in a man's world to lead interesting, useful, and profitable lives.

The anonymous communication was well written, blazing with conviction. But there was more than that to pique Mr. Madden's interest. It made sense.

The busy editor finally tossed it into the pile, finished the remainder of the mail, and went back to reading the tissue-paper slips bearing the telegraphic news. But when he had them impaled neatly on the nearby spindle, he took up the letter again. It intrigued him. He studied the handwriting. It appeared feminine, as feminine as the attitude it expressed. But surely no woman could write so logically and so eloquently.

He could not publish the thing, even with a signature. It was against his principles, against popular opinion. But he did want to know who had sent it. An idea came to him. He would advertise in the columns of the *Dispatch* for the writer's name and address, and, if he obtained them, he might assign a story to be written on the other side of the question. The author would turn out to be a man, of course, perhaps taking this way to attract attention and get a job. Madden would certainly give him one if he wrote like this consistently.

The advertisement appeared the next day. A reply came almost at once.

The letter was written by a woman. Her name was Elizabeth Cochrane, and she lived in Pittsburgh.

George Madden was a newspaperman by both training and instinct; he always followed a hunch. He wrote to Miss Cochrane and asked for an article on "Girls and Their Spheres in Life."

Again she was prompt; the article arrived within a few days. The editor read it and found it good. He paid for it. Then he abandoned caution. Fortifying himself, for he was positive he was opening the door to a battle-ax suffragette, he suggested that Elizabeth Cochrane might like to discuss further work for his paper. Elizabeth accepted a position as reporter for the *Dispatch*.

Elizabeth Cochrane, or Nellie Bly as she was also known, was born on May 5, 1867, in Armstrong County, Pennsylvania. According to friends and family, Nellie aspired to be more than what the stereotypical young girl was supposed to be. She liked traveling, adventure, and writing in-depth stories. She moved to Pittsburgh at the age of seventeen to pursue her dream of being an investigative reporter. Her first assignment for the *Dispatch* was to tackle the subject of divorce. She penned numerous articles for the paper ranging from conditions for workers in factories to the treatment of the mentally ill in asylums.

In 1887, Nellie moved to New York. It was there she met well-known publisher Joseph Pulitzer, and he hired her to work for his newspaper. Two years after starting the job at *World* newspaper she embarked on a journey that made her famous worldwide. Nellie wanted to go around the world in eighty days or less, and Pulitzer agreed to fund the intrepid reporter's venture.

Prior to Nellie beginning the trip, she ordered a couple of heavy dresses that could withstand constant wear for three months, and a light gown for the tropics. Those were the only dresses she took with her, but, in a small satchel and in a bag which she could sling over her shoulder, she placed a toothbrush, a light raincoat, flannel underwear, and a few other odds and ends.

On the morning of November 14, 1889, Nellie boarded the vessel the *Augusta Victoria*, one of the first steamers then passing between the United States and Europe. During her trip around the globe, she sent detailed reports of her travels that were published on the front page of the newspaper. In spite of the rapid pace she kept, she was able to interview several notable people in the countries through which she passed. Those articles were also carried by the newspaper.

Nellie Bly finished the trip in seventy-two days, six hours, eleven minutes, and fourteen seconds. She made a stop in France to meet with Jules Verne, author of *Around the World in 80 Days*.

In 1895, Nellie met millionaire Robert L. Seaman at a banquet in Chicago. Their marriage followed a few months after. He was seventy-five years old, and she was nearly thirty. He died a few years after they were wed, and Nellie inherited his fortune, although most of it was lost in litigation over the Ironclad Manufacturing Company, which was part of the estate.

Nellie Bly died of pneumonia on January 27, 1922, at St. Mark's Hospital in Manhattan. She is buried at the Woodland Cemetery in Bronx County, New York. She was fifty-seven when she passed away. The obituaries that ran in newspapers across the country remembered Nellie Bly as the "best reporter in America." Nellie's exploits were discussed and followed by curious readers from Independence, Missouri, to San Francisco, California. Initially, women were not involved in frontier journalism any more than they were in the front ranks of the Argonauts, the pioneers, lumberjacks, or construction crews. Nellie's work influenced many young women to pursue careers as journalists in the territory west of the Mississippi.

Seth Bullock

d. 1919

*[Seth Bullock is a] splendid-looking fellow with his size
and subtle strength, his strongly marked, aquiline face
with his big mustache, and the broad brim of his soft hat
drawn down around his hawk eyes.*

—PRESIDENT THEODORE ROOSEVELT

It wasn't a bullet from an outlaw's six-shooter or an enemy soldier in the Spanish-American War that claimed the life of one of the fiercest lawmen in the history of the Dakotas. Seth Bullock died of colon cancer. The accomplished businessman, rancher, politician, and lawman suffered with the disease for years and he died in September 1919 at the age of sixty-two. Born in Amhertberg, Ontario, Canada, in August 1876, six decades later he was remembered for his strength of character as well as the influence he had on the wild frontier.

According to the September 28, 1919, edition of the *Kansas City Star*, before Seth Bullock made his mark on the Black Hills of Dakota, he was a pioneer in Montana. He was the first sheriff in Helena, Montana, and a member of a famous vigilance committee that rid the region of a desperate band of horse thieves.

Seth Bullock COURTESY OF THE SOUTH DAKOTA STATE HISTORICAL SOCIETY

Seth Bullock's tombstone COURTESY DEADWOOD HISTORY, ADAMS MUSEUM COLLEC-
TION, DEADWOOD, SD

Upon hearing that gold had been discovered in the Black Hills, Seth and some of his friends decided to go to that area of the country in the summer of 1876. In March 1877, he became Lawrence County, Dakota's first sheriff. The gold camp contained some of the most notorious, cutthroat criminals in the country. Many were intimidated by the lawman.

Seth dressed like a minister, had the stare of a mad cobra, and was silent as a confidential clerk working for Rockefeller. In the beginning, his ability to effectively do his job in Lawrence County was challenged by an outlaw who intensely disliked the lawman. He gave orders that Seth should leave the camp and never return. The man threatened to shoot Seth if he didn't go. After being warned by friends, the sheriff borrowed a squirrel gun from an old hunter and proceeded down the street to the saloon where the desperado was waiting. When the man saw Seth unafraid and coming right for him, he backed down and fled the scene.

As a representative of law and order, the Dakota lawman tracked down a number of stage robbers, gamblers, and murderers, and, according to the October 1, 1919, edition of the *Fort Wayne Journal Gazette*, killed more than twenty-five lawbreakers who refused arrest.

In addition to his career in law enforcement (Seth also served as a US marshal in Western Dakota Territory) he co-owned and operated a hardware store and warehouse in Deadwood with his business partner Sol Star. It was one of the most prosperous companies in the Black Hills.

Seth met Theodore Roosevelt in 1884. Roosevelt was a deputy sheriff in Medora, North Dakota, and had tracked a criminal to Seth's jurisdiction. The two lawmen became fast friends. He became one of Roosevelt's Rough Riders in the Spanish-American War and was named captain of one of the future president's troops.

Seth was an elected representative to the Senate and introduced the resolution to set aside Yellowstone as a national park. He was the first forest supervisor of the Black Hills and the cofounder of the mining town Belle Fourche.

Seth was serving his third term as US marshal for the District of South Dakota when he was diagnosed with cancer. Friends and family noted that in spite of his health he refused to be complacent. He continued on with his work regardless of the debilitating illness.

When President Roosevelt died in January 1919, Seth decided to erect a monument in his friend's honor. He oversaw the building of a stone tower known as Mount Roosevelt on Sheep Mountain located five miles from Deadwood. The tower was completed in June 1919. Seth died on September 23, 1919, at his home surrounded by his loved ones. He was buried at Mount Moriah Cemetery in Deadwood. His grave faces Mount Roosevelt.

Cattle Annie and Little Britches

d. 1978 and ?

A deputy marshal and a posse arrested two notorious
female outlaws. ... One was in men's clothing.

—AUGUST 21, 1895 EDITION OF *EVENING GAZETTE*,
CEDAR RAPIDS, IOWA

On the afternoon of August 18, 1895, US Marshal Bill Tilghman and Deputy Marshal Steve Burke led their horses toward a small farm outside Pawnee, Oklahoma. The lawmen had tracked a pair of outlaws to the location and were proceeding cautiously when several gunshots were fired.

Marshall Tilghman caught sight of a Winchester rifle sticking out a broken window of a dilapidated cabin. He spurred his horse out of the line of fire just as the weapon went off. He steered his mount around the building and arrived at the back door the same time sixteen-year-old Jennie Stevens, alias Little Britches, burst out of the house. She shot at him with a pistol while racing to a horse waiting nearby.

By the time Marshal Tilghman settled his ride and drew his weapon, Jennie was on her horse. She turned the horse away from the cabin, kicked it hard in the ribs, and the animal took

Cattle Annie and Little Britches RESEARCH DIVISION OF THE OKLAHOMA HISTORICAL
SOCIETY

off. Tilghman leveled his firearm at the woman and shot. Jennie's
horse stumbled and fell, and she was tossed from the animal's back,
losing her gun in the process.

The marshal hopped off his own ride and hurried over to the
stunned and annoyed runaway. Jennie picked herself up quickly

and cursed her misfortune. She charged the lawman, dug her fingernails into his neck, and slapped him several times before he could subdue her. He was a battered man when he finally pinned her arms behind her back.

Back at the cabin, Deputy Marshal Steve Burke wrestled a gun away from thirteen-year-old Annie McDoulet, alias Cattle Annie, a rail-thin young woman wearing a gingham dress and a black, wide-brimmed straw hat. The pistol she had tried to shoot him with was lying in the dirt several feet in front of her.

Two years prior to their apprehension and arrest, Cattle Annie and Little Britches were riding with the Doolin gang, a notorious band of outlaws who robbed trains and banks. Enamored of the fame of the well-known criminals, the teenage girls had decided to leave home and follow the bandits. They helped the criminals steal cattle, horses, guns, and ammunition and warned them whenever law enforcement was on their trail.

Legend tells that Bill Doolin, leader of the Doolin gang, gave Cattle Annie and Little Britches their nicknames. Cattle Annie was born Anna Emmaline McDoulet in Kansas in 1882. Jennie Stevenson was born in 1879 in Oklahoma. Both girls had run afoul of the law before joining the Doolin gang. Each sold whiskey to Osage Indians. According to the September 3, 1895, edition of the Ada, Oklahoma, newspaper the *Evening Times*, Jennie seemed to have "plied her vocation for a long time successfully, going in the guise of a boy tramp hunting work." In between selling liquor to Indians and life with the Doolins, Jennie had married a deaf mute named Midkiff and Annie rustled livestock.

News of Cattle Annie and Little Britches' arrest was reported in the August 21, 1895, edition of the Cedar Rapids, Iowa, newspaper the *Evening Gazette*. "A deputy marshal and a posse arrested two notorious female outlaws but had to fight to make the arrest," the article read. "The marshal's posse ran into them and they showed fight. Several shots were fired before they gave up. One was in men's clothing."

The teenage outlaws were held in the jail in Guthrie, Oklahoma Territory, until a trial was held. They were found guilty of horse stealing and sentenced to ten years' imprisonment at the Farmington Reform School in Massachusetts. Cattle Annie and Little Britches were model prisoners and only served three years of their sentence.

Annie returned to Oklahoma Territory, where she met and married Earl Frost in March 1901. The couple divorced after eight years. In 1912 Annie married a house painter and general contractor named Whitmore R. Roach. They had two sons and lived a respectable life in Oklahoma City. Annie McDoulet Frost Roach died from natural causes on November 7, 1978, at the age of ninety-five. Her obituary ran in the November 8, 1978, edition of the Oklahoma City newspaper the *Oklahoman*. The article noted that "she was a retired bookkeeper and member of the American Legion Auxiliary and the Olivet Baptist Church. She had five grandchildren and thirteen great-grandchildren. She was laid to rest at Rose Hill Burial Park in Oklahoma City."

Little Britches returned to Oklahoma, as well. She married, raised a family, and lived a life of quiet domesticity in Tulsa. How long she lived and where she passed away are both unknown.

John Chisum

d. 1884

No matter where people go, sooner or later there's the law.
And sooner or later they find God's already been there.

—JOHN WAYNE AS JOHN CHISUM IN *CHISUM* (1970)

Cattle barons of the vast frontier such as John Chisum once held undisputed sway over the great public domain. He ruled like a lord of old over the Pecos country in New Mexico where desperate battles were fought between rival cattle barons for more grazing land.

Rancher John Simpson Chisum was born into an affluent family in Tennessee on a plantation on August 16, 1824. His parents relocated their five children to Red River County, Texas, in 1837. John was thirteen when his family settled in Paris, Texas. He worked a series of odd jobs before becoming the county clerk in 1852.

At the age of thirty, John ventured into cattle ranching with Stephen K. Fowler, a businessman from New York. The Half Circle P brand, owned by Chisum and Fowler, was seen on livestock across a great expanse of the land John purchased in Denton County, Texas. Stephen's original investment of $6,000 resulted in a $100,000 profit in ten years.

Chisum used his portion of profitable shares to buy more land and cattle. In addition to running his own spread, which included five thousand head of cattle, John also managed livestock for other ranchers and ambitious investors. By 1861, John Chisum was recognized as one of the most important cattle dealers in North Texas.

When the Civil War started, John contracted with the military to supply beef to soldiers in the Trans-Mississippi Confederate Army Department. After the war he drove his cattle into eastern New Mexico to sell to the government for the cavalry and the Indian reservations. In 1867, John moved his base of operation to Roswell, New Mexico, where he already had more than one thousand head of cows. He established a series of ranches along a 150-mile stretch of the Pecos River. John's empire grew to eighty thousand head of cattle and he hired more than one hundred cowboys to work the livestock.

John Chisum was involved tangentially with the Lincoln County Range War in 1878. The dispute initially began as a fight between cattlemen and two store owners over who rightfully controlled the trade of dry goods in the county. Cattlemen John Tunstall and his business partner, Alexander McSween, owned one of the stores, and they were being threatened by the owners of the competing establishment who had an economic stranglehold on the area. Each store owner organized his own men to protect his enterprises and homes from being overrun. Tunstall and McSween had in their employ Billy the Kid and his associates. John Chisum supported Tunstall's efforts. His exact role in the dispute is unknown.

After Tunstall was murdered, Billy the Kid took Chisum to task over money he insisted John owed him for protection. Chisum disagreed, and Billy resented him for it. In 1880, Chisum helped get Pat Garrett, the sheriff who shot Billy the Kid, elected to office.

John Chisum's cattle operations continued to thrive, and he shared his good fortune with his brother, James. John gave James his own herd of cattle to manage.

John Chisum's tombstone LAMAR COUNTY HISTORICAL MUSEUM

John contracted throat cancer in late 1883 and had surgery to remove the growth in 1884. He died on December 22, 1884, in Eureka, Arkansas, where he had been recuperating from the operation. His giant cattle empire was worth $500,000. Chisum never married, but it is believed he fathered two children with one of the slave women he owned named Jensie.

John Chisum's body was laid to rest in Paris, Texas. He was sixty years old when he passed away.

Stephen Foster

d. 1864

Now the nodding wild flow'rs may wither on the shore
While her gentle fingers will cull them no more
Oh! I sigh for Jeannie with the light brown hair
Floating like a vapor, on the soft summer air

—FROM "JEANNIE WITH THE LIGHT BROWN HAIR"
BY STEPHEN FOSTER

Songwriter and composer Stephen Collins Foster was lying face down in a pool of his own blood when a housekeeper at a cheap New York boarding house found him on the morning of January 13, 1864. The man who had penned such popular tunes as "Oh! Susanna" and "Jeannie with the Light Brown Hair" collapsed from a fever while walking to a wash basin to get some water. He struck his head on the porcelain bowl and cut a large gash in his face and neck. He was taken to Bellevue Hospital where he was pronounced dead.

Stephen Foster was born on July 4, 1826, in Lawrenceville, Pennsylvania. He was the youngest of eleven children and from an early age displayed exceptional musical talent. At seven years old his parents gave him a flageolet, a sixteenth-century woodwind

Stephen Foster LIBRARY OF CONGRESS LC_USZ62-56944

instrument. Within a short time, Stephen mastered the flute-like whistle and expanded his abilities to include harmonica, piano, and guitar. Although his talent captivated family and friends, he did not have a desire to perform. Stephen preferred to write and wanted to study music as a science.

In 1841 Stephen's mother hired a tutor to teach her son the fundamentals of music as well as how to speak French and

German. Stephen composed his first published song, entitled "Open Thy Lattice Love," in 1842 at the age of seventeen. A short time later he moved to Cincinnati, Ohio, and took a job working for his brother as an accounting clerk. He wrote many more songs during this time, all of which were published, but the money he received for his work was next to nothing.

By 1850 he decided to abandon the accounting business and devote himself full-time to writing music. His gift for harmony and poetry led to the creation of such well-known tunes as "Camptown Races" and "My Old Kentucky Home." During this time he met Jane McDowell, the daughter of a physician from the Pittsburgh area. The two fell in love and were married July 22, 1850. Stephen continued writing songs that were published and well received, but he realized very little financially for his music because of weak copyright laws. Unfortunately, multiple publishers often printed their own competing editions of Stephen's songs, paying him nothing and eroding any long-term monetary benefits.

Stephen's struggles with managing his money and the loss of his parents as well as many of his siblings in a short time period proved more than he could bear. Consequently he sought comfort in drinking. The alcohol soon became all-consuming and quickly became an issue in his marriage. Stephen became addicted and after numerous ultimatums and attempts to get him to stop drinking, Jane decided to take their daughter back to her parents' home in Pittsburgh.

Stephen sank into a deep depression and continued drinking. He spent all his income on alcohol, and when he ran out of money he sold his clothing to buy more to drink. He wore rags and went days without eating. His brothers and sister would step in to help, but Stephen would not and could not change. On Saturday evening, January 9, 1864, the thirty-seven-year-old man passed out in a drunken stupor in his hotel room. When he awoke, he was violently ill from liver failure and in his weakened condition he fell and hit his head.

Stephen's wife Jane and one of his brothers came to the hospital to claim his body. Nurses gave his family his clothes along with 38 cents that were found in his pocket and a scrap of paper upon which he had written the words, "Dear Friends and Gentle Hearts."

He was buried in Alleghany Cemetery in Pittsburgh, beside his mother. Upon his plain marble headstone is the simple inscription: "Stephen Foster of Pittsburgh. Born July 4, 1826. Died January 13, 1864."

Jessie Fremont

d. 1902

Mrs. Frémont was a remarkable woman, to whom the territory west of the Mississippi River owes more than to any other person perhaps in the country. She helped bring about the preservation of more than twelve hundred square miles of land in Northern California known as Yosemite. She wielded an influence second to but few statesmen of her generation.

—FORT WAYNE EVENING SENTINEL, DECEMBER 29, 1902

On December 27, 1902, the woman many historians referred to as the "Guardian of Yosemite National Park" passed away. Jessie Anne Benton Fremont was born on May 31, 1824, in the Blue Ridge Mountains of Virginia. Her father, Thomas Hart Benton, was an ambitious man who went from farming into politics and eventually became a US senator from Missouri (and great-uncle of twentieth-century muralist Thomas Hart Benton). Jessie visited Washington, D.C., often as a child and met with such luminaries as President Andrew Jackson and Congressman Davy Crockett.

Jessie and her sister, Elizabeth, attended the capital's leading girl's boarding school, alongside the daughters of other political

Jessie Benton Fremont LIBRARY OF CONGRESS LC_USZ62-44060

leaders and wealthy business owners. It was for that very reason Jessie disliked school. "There was no end to the conceit, the assumption, the class distinction there," she wrote in her memoirs. In addition to the lines drawn between the children of various social standings, Jessie felt the studies were not challenging to her. "I was miserable in the narrow, elitist atmosphere. I learned nothing there," she recalled in her journal. The best thing about attending school was the opportunity it afforded her to meet John Fremont, the man who would become her husband.

Born on January 21, 1813, John was an intelligent, attractive man with gray-blue eyes who excelled in mathematics and craved adventure. While awaiting an assignment from the US Corps of Topographical Engineers (a war department agency engaged in exploring and mapping unknown regions of the United States), John was introduced to Thomas Benton. Benton was a key proponent in Washington for western expeditions. He and John discussed the great need for the land west of the Missouri River to be explored. Benton invited the young surveyor and mapmaker to continue the conversation at his home over a meal with his family. It was there that Jessie and John first met, and they were instantly smitten with each other. Within a year, they were wed.

Jessie Benton was sixteen years old and John Fremont was twenty-seven when they married on October 19, 1841. The newlyweds lived at the Gatsby Hotel on Capitol Hill until John was assigned to lead a four-month expedition to the Rocky Mountains. Jessie helped him prepare for the journey by reviewing information about the plant life, Indian encampments, and rock formations he would come in contact with during his trip. John headed west on May 2, 1842. Jessie, who was pregnant with their first child, moved into a small apartment near her parents' home.

John returned to Washington, D.C., in November 1842, just two weeks before their daughter was born. He watched over baby Elizabeth Benton "Lily" Fremont while Jessie reviewed the slim notes John had taken during the expedition and fashioned a report for the government using his data and detailed recollections of life on the trail. Politicians such as Missouri senator Lewis Linn praised the report for being not only practical and informative but entertaining as well. The material would be used by emigrants as a guidebook.

In early 1843, John moved his family to St. Louis, Missouri, where his next expedition would be originating. Jessie took on the role as John's secretary, reviewing mail from suppliers and frontiersmen such as Kit Carson. She wrote the necessary correspondence to members of the Topographical Bureau, apprising them of the date the expedition would begin, how long it would take, and what the party planned to accomplish. Shortly before John departed to explore a route to the Pacific Coast, a letter came to the Fremonts' home instructing him to postpone the expedition until questions over a request to purchase weapons had been settled. Fearing the entire mission would be jeopardized if the journey was delayed, Jessie did not give the letter to her husband. John set out on the expedition on May 13, 1843. He returned home the following August, having successfully begun opening up the great territory between the Mississippi Valley and California.

Jessie again translated the notes and stories about John's venture into a captivating narrative. The report was widely circulated and prompted numerous people to move to California and Oregon in search of a better life. The government approved a third expedition over the Rocky Mountains. Between May 1845 and 1849, John would trek back and forth from his home with Jessie and his daughter to the Pacific Coast two more times. He uncovered new and better routes to an area many pioneers referred to as a "veritable paradise."

In May 1849, Jessie and her daughter traveled to San Francisco to join John already in California. The seaport town was crowded with people who had heard rumors that there was gold in the hills around Sacramento. John wasn't interested in prospecting. But because lumber was in great demand, he decided to invest in a sawmill. The investment proved to be a wise one. The mill made a substantial profit in a short amount of time. John used a portion of his earnings to purchase a large ranch near Yosemite.

Jesse spent her time in the Sierras tending to her family and writing about the beauty and dangers of life in Yosemite. The cold mountain weather adversely affected Jessie's health, however, and her lungs were weak. In the fall of 1849, the Fremonts moved to Monterey.

In December 1849, John was named the Democratic candidate for the US Senate. The following year he was sworn into the post. Jessie proved to be a capable politician's wife. She hosted delegate meetings and spoke out against slavery and why California should be admitted to the Union as a free state. Jessie's influence and John's perseverance played major roles in bringing about that outcome. On December 9, 1850, California became the thirty-first state.

In 1853, Congress approved several confidential routes between the thirty-second and forty-seventh parallels. John was hired to help map out a passage for the Pacific Railroad.

After John's two failed attempts to run for the office of president of the United States and embarking on several more survey missions, the Fremonts returned to their home near Yosemite in 1858.

Horace Greely, the famous political activist and editor of the *New York Tribune*, visited the Fremonts at their Bear Valley home in the spring of 1859. It was Horace's first trip to the far west, and, he, like many other well-known individuals who saw Yosemite, was just as captivated by the spectacular setting as Jessie. Jessie shared with Horace that her time in Bear Valley had been "better than all the days of my life." It was her description of Yosemite and the time spent living there that helped persuade Congress to set aside thousands of acres of the Yosemite Valley and the neighboring Mariposa Grove of big trees (now officially the Mariposa Grove of Giant Sequoias) to someday be used as a national park.

In 1864, Jessie called together several influential people who had visited her and her family during their time in Yosemite, including Greely; minister and politician Thomas Starr King; US Senator Edward Baker of Oregon; a representative for the Central American Steam Transit Company, Israel Ward Raymond; and journalist and landscape designer Frederick Law Olmsted, to compile photographs, sketches, and research material of the area to be presented to President Abraham Lincoln. She hoped the information would help persuade the president to protect the picturesque valley from mining and lumber companies who wanted to take over the land. Some of the natural marvels Jessie and the cohort of people she enlisted to research, paint, and photograph were Half Dome, a stone mountain on the eastern side of Yosemite; El Capitan, a smooth slab of rocks more than 3,600 feet high that stands guard near the valley entrance; and the lovely, wispy, wind-blown Bridalveil Falls. Israel Raymond drafted the letter that explained in detail the vital need to protect the wonders of Yosemite. On June 30, 1864, President Lincoln signed a bill that made certain Yosemite would be held "for public use, resort, and recreation for all time."

From 1878 to 1881, Jessie and John lived in Prescott, Arizona, while John served as governor of the territory. Jessie helped support the family by writing stories for various magazines, including a publication for children entitled *Wide Awake*. In 1890 the book she penned about her life in California, specifically her time in the Yosemite Valley, was published. *Far-West Sketches* was a popular seller among travelers to the Sierra Foothills. That same year, John died suddenly of peritonitis.

Jessie returned to California from New York, where she and John had been living at the time of his death. She dealt with the grief of losing John by completing several of his unfinished writings. Those articles were later published in *Century Magazine*.

Yosemite officially became a national park on October 1, 1890.

On Christmas Day 1902, twelve years after Yosemite came into providence, Jessie Fremont collapsed from pneumonia. She grew steadily worse and lapsed into unconsciousness from which she never rallied. She died in her home in Los Angeles surrounded by her three children. She was seventy-eight years old. Although there is currently no monument to recognize her life or work, Congress is currently considering a bill that would rename Yosemite Peak after the nineteenth-century preservationist.

Pat Garrett

d. 1908

I at once recognized the man and knew he was the Kid, and reached behind me for my pistol. . . . I pulled the trigger and he received his death wound, for the ball struck him in the left breast and pierced his heart. He never spoke, but died in a minute.

—Pat Garrett's written account to the governor of New Mexico on the shooting of Billy the Kid

Patrick Floyd Jarvis Garrett is remembered best for being the man who shot Billy the Kid, but his contribution to taming the American West consisted of much more than that single event. For more than eighteen years, the US lawman tracked down numerous outlaws running wild along the Texas–New Mexico border.

He was born on June 5, 1850, in Chambers County, Alabama. When he was three years old, his parents, John and Elizabeth, purchased a plantation in Louisiana and moved their children to their new home near the town of Haynesville, Alabama. At the age of nineteen the six-foot-four-inch Pat struck out on his own and made his way to the Texas Panhandle. He signed on with a team of ranchers driving herds of cattle to market. He later left work to become a buffalo hunter.

The first gunfight Garrett was involved in occurred in November 1876 in Fort Griffith, Texas. A heated exchange with a buffalo skinner over some hides resulted in a fistfight and further escalated to gunplay. Garrett, who was an excellent marksman, shot the man in the chest.

Shortly after the incident he departed Texas and rode into New Mexico where he became a cowpuncher for a Lincoln County rancher. During his employment as a ranch hand there, he met and married a young woman named Juanita Gutierrez. Within a year after they wed, his bride died. He later married Juanita's sister Apolinaria, and the couple had nine children.

In 1878, Garrett had traded in his job as a cowboy to become a saloon owner. He catered to the rough range riders, serving not only drinks but food as well. When Garrett wasn't tending bar, he was gambling and dealing faro to his customers. William H. Bonney, better known as Billy the Kid, was a frequent patron. Pat and Billy got along very well together and became fast friends. The two men swapped stories of the rough life on the frontier. Billy trusted Pat and regarded him as an older brother. Because both liked to gamble, the pair gave each other the nicknames of Little Casino and Big Casino. Garrett knew the Kid's hideouts and his partners in crime. It was in part Garrett's friendship with the Kid that prompted territory officials to appoint Garrett to the post of sheriff. His background as a reformed gunfighter and his familiarity with the notorious outlaw made him a natural for the job.

Garrett was sworn in as the Lincoln County sheriff on November 7, 1880. The war between the cattle barons and Billy the Kid was in full swing. The Kid and his friends had shot and killed several of the gunmen hired by the cattle barons to kill John Tunstall. Tunstall had been the Kid's employer and mentor. Garrett's job was to put an end to the conflict and arrest Billy and his cohorts.

The sheriff and his deputies took off after the fugitive and caught up with him in late December. The Kid was taken into custody and escorted to the town of Mesilla to stand trial. Billy was convicted on murder charges and sentenced to be hanged. But days before the punishment was to be enforced, the Kid escaped in a hail of gunfire.

Garrett formed another posse and rode to Fort Sumner following a tip that the Kid was hiding with his friends at the army post. On July 15, 1881, under the cover of darkness, Sheriff Garrett and his men snuck into the compound and surprised the Kid. Before the outlaw could draw his weapon, Garrett fired his own gun twice and killed him.

The news that Pat Garrett had brought down the notorious Billy the Kid spread quickly across the West and brought the key players in the shootout instant fame. Because of Pat's previous affiliation with the young renegade and the sympathy he had for Billy's desperate situation, some historians question Garrett's account of the Kid's demise and maintain he escaped. The debate has kept people interested in the lawman and outlaw for decades.

Garrett finished his term as sheriff in 1882, and then turned his attention to ranching and politics. In 1884 he made an unsuccessful run for the New Mexico state senate as well as a bid for the Republican nomination to serve another two years as sheriff. Garrett returned to Texas to work as a ranger and achieved the rank of captain in the corps.

From 1885 to 1896 the restless lawman traveled back and forth between New Mexico and Texas several times. He held various high-profile jobs in both places, including serving as county commissioner in Uvalde County, Texas, and sheriff of Dona Ana County, New Mexico. In 1901 President Theodore Roosevelt appointed him as customs inspector in El Paso. After holding the position for five years, he retired to his ranch in Las Cruces, New Mexico.

Pat Garrett's tombstone COURTESY OF PEGGY WOOD

On February 29, 1908, Garrett was involved in a feud over land he had leased to a farmer. Garrett objected to the farmer's goats grazing on acreage he believed should be for cattle only. The minor range war sparked a deadly outcome. One of the men Garrett had argued with ambushed him and shot him in the back of the head when the famous ex-sheriff had stopped to relieve himself.

The former lawman's lifeless body was left on the side of the road until Las Cruces sheriff Felipe Lucero arrived on the scene four hours later and identified the dead man. Garrett's tall frame would not fit in an average-sized coffin of five-feet-five inches, so a special casket had to be made for him. After his body was placed inside the coffin, he was put on display at Strong's Undertaking Parlor.

The funeral for Pat Garrett was held on March 5, 1908, and was attended by hundreds of southern New Mexico residents. The graveside service included a eulogy from Garrett's longtime friend and well-known gambler, Tom Powers. Pat Garrett was laid to rest beside his daughter, Ida, at the Masonic Cemetery in Las Cruces, New Mexico. The cemetery is located on 760 S. Compress Road in Dona Ana County.

The cattleman who shot and killed Garrett later confessed to the murder. The judge who presided over the man's hearing had disliked Garrett because he felt he was arrogant. His bias prompted him to rule that the rancher had acted in self-defense, and the man was acquitted.

Mary Graves

d. 1891

"Even the wind seemed to hold its breath as the suggestion was made that were one to die, the rest might live," said *Mary Ann Graves.*

—THE PERILOUS JOURNEY OF THE DONNER PARTY,
BY MARIAN CALABRO

If Mary Graves had stayed in Indiana where she was born on November 1, 1826, she might very well have married the boy next door, taught students to read and write at a schoolhouse in her hometown, and lived out her days watching her children and grandchildren grow up on the family farm. Her life, however, took a different course when her family joined the Donner Party in 1846 and headed west.

Mary was nineteen when her father, Franklin, made the decision to move his family to California. The wagon train the Graves joined was organized by George and Jacob Donner and James Reed and their families. The initial group set out from Springfield, Illinois, in April and was joined by additional members when it reached Independence, Missouri.

Mary Graves

Franklin and Elizabeth Graves and their nine children joined the Donner Party in August at Fort Bridger, Wyoming, with their belongings piled in three large wagons.

Mary was excited about the journey. She had no doubt heard stories of the golden land of opportunity and couldn't wait to see its riches for herself. She knew her family might experience difficulties getting there but that had not put a damper on her gleeful spirit. She didn't care that the trail was treacherous, and she wasn't afraid of the Indians that guarded the way. She placed all her faith in God and her father to get her and her family to their new home safely.

Historical records note that Mary was a beautiful young lady with dark eyes and long, wavy black hair. She carried her slender, five-foot-seven-inch frame with grace. Her complexion was creamy olive. She captured the attention of many of the twenty-two single men in the party, but she was engaged to John Snyder, the driver of one of her father's teams.

It was October 5, 1846, when John Snyder and Milton Elliott, another driver, exchanged heated words over whose team of oxen could pull a load faster. John's and Milton's teams got tangled up as they raced each other to the top of the hill. John was furious and started cussing at Milton and beating his livestock with a whipstock. James Reed stepped in and attempted to calm him down. John thought James was threatening him, and he jumped off his wagon and beat James over the head with the butt end of his heavy whipstock while Mary looked on. When James Reed managed to stand up and wipe the blood from his eyes, his wife ran over to help him, and John hit her over the head too. James quickly pulled out a knife and stabbed John. Mary's intended died fifteen minutes later. The stunned onlookers were outraged. They wanted to hang James. Mary was asked to sit in judgment of him, but she refused. James was banished from the group.

The gleam in Mary's eyes had started to fade. The journey west was grueling. In addition to having battled the heat and rough terrain, the party had taken a "shortcut" to California that actually took them several hundred miles out of their way. The combination of lack of water and a variety of petty arguments—like the one between John, Milton, and James—created strife among the party members. Their food was running low and many of their oxen and horses had been stolen by Indians.

Mary and the others finally reached the Sierra Nevada Mountains on October 28, 1846.

This final pass usually brought joy to weary emigrants. It brought terror and dismay to the Donner Party. They could see dark skies ahead. Soon the winter storm clouds dumped six inches of snow on the travelers. They were trapped; the snow prevented them from going any further.

The emigrants quickly built crude cabins near a lake to protect them from the cold. Mary's family shared their tiny makeshift home with another large family in the party. Food was scarce. Time passed and the snow continued to fall.

By mid-December, Mary, her father, and Charles Stanton realized they would have to organize a team and go for help. Fifteen members of the group, including Mary, her father, her sister, her brother-in-law, and two Indian guides volunteered to be a part of the party and make their way over the summit to Sutter's Fort.

Wearing snowshoes made from oxbows and cowhide and carrying enough provisions to last six days, the "Forlorn Hope" party set off. They soon encountered snowdrifts that varied in depth from twelve to sixty feet. The fifteen traveled without saying a word, their eyes fixed on the ground. The fatigue and dazzling sunlight made some of them, such as Charles Stanton, snow-blind. Every day, Charles fell farther and farther behind the others. On the third day, Charles staggered into camp long after the others had finished their meager meal. He never complained but struggled daily to keep pace with the others. Mary's heart broke for him.

On the fifth morning, the members of the Forlorn Hope set out, leaving Charles behind at the smoldering campfire, smoking a cigarette. All day long Mary kept looking back to see if Charles had caught up with the party. By the day's end, she knew he wasn't coming. Indeed, Charles Stanton had died.

Mary's father and two other men were the next to die. Before Franklin Graves passed away, he called his daughters to his side. "You have to do whatever you can to stay alive. Think of your mother and brothers and sisters in the cabin at the lake. If you don't make it to Sutter's Fort, and send help, everyone at the lake will die. I want you to do what you have to. . . . Use my flesh to stay alive." The mere thought of doing such a thing made the girls cry, but they knew he was right. They would have to resort to cannibalism to survive.

The remaining eleven members of the Forlorn Hope party sat down in the snow to discuss whether to go ahead without provisions, or go back to the cabins, where they must undoubtedly starve. Some of those who had children and families wished to go back, but the two Indians said they would go on to Sutter's Fort. Mary opted to continue on, too, and the others agreed.

As the party traveled on together, another furious storm bombarded the Sierras. More men died and the women were weakening. It had been twelve days since the rescue team had left their loved ones and friends at the cabins. They had walked so many miles that their feet were bleeding. They were starving and cold.

One morning Mary and fellow party member William Eddy struck out together to find food. They had gone two miles when they noticed a place where a deer had slept the night before. The two burst into tears at the hope of finding the animal. They dropped to their knees to pray. When they sighted the buck, William fired his rifle at it. The deer continued running. The deer dropped into the snow and the pair raced toward it. William cut a deep V in its throat, and the two fell on the animal and drank the warm blood.

Within a few days, there was nothing left of the deer and starvation again set in. Only five women and two men now remained. The feeble party traveled on day after day. Their strength was almost gone when someone noticed tracks in the snow. The group followed the tracks until they came in full view of a Washo Indian camp. The Indian women and children stared in amazement at the skeleton-like figures that came into their camp. They quickly fed the starving group and tended to their battered feet and other wounds. It had been thirty-two days since the party had left the lake.

Mary Graves no longer looked the way she did when the journey began. Her high cheekbones were grotesquely prominent and her cheeks were buried deep below them. Her eyes were dim and sunken. Her once-perfect skin now had the appearance of baked leather. With good food and much care, her looks would be restored, but her spirit would never be the same.

Relief parties from Sutter's Fort rescued Mary's family and the rest of the surviving members of the Donner Party in April. Mary's mother and five-year-old brother had died. Mary and her sister Sarah were now in charge of their younger siblings.

The forty-six remaining members of the party were escorted to Sutter's Fort. The horrific tales of survival they relayed to the inquisitive people who gathered around them brought tears to their eyes. Mary's once cheerful disposition had now been replaced

Mary Graves Clarke's grave marker COURTESY TERRY OMMEN

with a despondent nature. She thrived on the stories told about her mother in her last days. Mary's mother was praised by the survivors for her charity. She was a generous woman who gave all she had to give. Mary was inspired by her mother's actions, and it spurred her on despite her depression.

On May 16, 1847, Mary married Edward Pyle, a member of the relief expedition that went to the aid of the Donner Party. The couple left Sutter's Fort with her brother and sisters and settled in the San Jose area. It was here she entered the teaching profession. Her career was interrupted when Edward disappeared while on a business trip in Tulare County, California. Mary's search for her husband ended after a year, when his murdered body was discovered near Tulare Lake.

Antonio Valencia was tried and convicted for the crime. Valencia had dragged Edward one hundred yards at the end of his rope and then cut Edward's throat. His body was shot full of arrows to give the impression that his death was the result of an Indian attack.

Valencia was sentenced to be hanged and Mary was determined that justice would be served. On the off chance a vigilante group would try to kill him, either by poisoning or shooting him before the execution date, Mary went to the prison every day and prepared the murderer's meals.

In 1852, Mary married a sheep rancher named J. T. Clarke and they moved to a town near the White River in Tulare County. She became the region's first schoolteacher, educating generations of children, including the six she and J. T. had.

Mary always stayed close to her home. Other members of the Donner Party eventually returned to the "place of horror" as Mary called it, but she never did.

Mary Anna Graves Clarke died of pneumonia in Traver, Tulare County, on March 9, 1891. Her twenty-six-year-old son had been struggling with the same ailment for several days. He passed away four days prior to his mother. Mary was sixty-five years old when she died. She is buried at the Visalia Public Cemetery in Tulare County.

Agnes Lake Hickok

d. 1907

[Agnes Lake] made a higher ascent on a wire than any
performer of her day in 1858.

—*New York Times*, August 23, 1907

Wild Bill Hickok had many female admirers in his lifetime, but
Agnes Lake Thatcher was the only woman who completely captured his heart. The man known as the "deadliest pistolero in the
Old West" often declared to his friends that he preferred being
a bachelor. It was a surprise to many when he married a widow
several years older than himself. The circumstances that resulted in
so great a change were romantically singular and worthy of record.

Mrs. Hickok was born Agnes Louise Messman on August 23,
1826, in Eastern Alsace, France. Her mother died when she was four
years old, and, shortly thereafter, her father took Agnes to America.
The Messmans settled in Cincinnati, Ohio, when she was sixteen years
old. As a child Agnes was an avid horseback rider. Her father helped
mold her remarkable skill into a circus routine. In 1841, Agnes met
a circus clown named William Lake Thatcher. He was a native New
Yorker and used his connections to secure a job for Agnes with the
circus he worked for, the Spaulding and Rogers Circus.

Agnes Lake

In addition to displaying impressive equestrian abilities, Agnes performed daring feats of skill on a tightrope. By 1859, she was billed the "queen of the high wire" and the most famous equestrienne the American circus had ever known.

Although her father disapproved of William Lake Thatcher because of his profession and the vagabond lifestyle that went with the job, Agnes married him anyway. The pair wed in Louisiana in August 1842. William dropped the name of Thatcher so his and his bride's names would fit on the advertisement for the circus. Billed as Bill and Agnes Lake, the couple worked for Spaulding and Rogers for more than ten years. During that time they saved much of the money they earned with the hopes of starting a circus of their own. Their dream was partially realized in 1860 when Lake formed a partnership with veteran circus man John Robinson. The show was known as the Robinson Lake Circus. William and Agnes devoted six years to the venture, then moved to their own production. During the time the pair had a daughter they named Emma.

At the conclusion of the first season of the Lake Circus, Agnes had toured all of Europe in an equestrian-themed play entitled *Mazeppa*. Back in the States, Lake's troupe spent three years performing in various locations from Syracuse, New York, to Independence, Missouri. Thirty-five wagons transported the show from town to town.

In mid-1869, the Lake Circus returned to Granby, Missouri, and then traveled west as far as Abilene, Kansas. During the Lakes' stay in Abilene, William got into an altercation with a man named Jake Killian (some historical records spell the last name Gillen). The Cheyenne, Wyoming, newspaper the *Cheyenne Daily Leader* reported that Killian had sneaked into the circus tent and was trying to see the show without paying. William confronted him, the two men argued, and William kicked Killian out of the tent. Killian was furious. He pulled a gun out of his pocket and shot William in the head, killing him instantly.

Agnes halted the show's run long enough to bury her husband and get her financial affairs in order. She then reassembled the circus troupe and continued on with a series of scheduled performances. Lake Circus did well under Agnes's direction. She proved to be not only a talented performer but also a smart businesswoman. By 1872 she had earned a substantial amount from touring and decided to sell the show to a competitor. She used the funds from the sale to invest in a lithograph business in Cincinnati. A serious economic downturn brought on by the severe drop in demand for silver plunged the United States and Europe into a major depression. Agnes lost everything and was forced to return to the circus.

Bill Hickok, who had met Agnes in Kansas in 1869, was quite taken with the fearless founder of Lake Circus; he wrote her to express his concern for her well-being and share with her what was happening in his life since they last saw one another in Kansas. The two then began regularly corresponding.

In 1874, Agnes and Bill's paths converged in Rochester, New York. Bill was there with the Buffalo Bill Cody western show, and Agnes was in the city working for the Great Eastern Circus. According to the Des Moines, Iowa, newspaper the *Tribune*, dated August 29, 1929, it was during this time that Bill told Agnes he was in love with her and asked her to marry him. Until Emma was grown and settled into a profession or married, Agnes did not feel she could commit to his proposal. It wasn't until Agnes's daughter Emma married in 1875 in Cincinnati that the chance presented itself for Bill and Agnes to see one another again. This time the two were in Cheyenne, Wyoming.

Bill was making final arrangements to travel to the Black Hills of Dakota to search for gold. Agnes was in town visiting relatives. When Bill learned she was in Cheyenne, he hurried to see her. "Wild Bill then renewed his suit," the *Tribune* article noted, "and pressed his claims with such persistency that the engagement was perfected and arrangements concluded for the wedding, which it was agreed would take place on the following day."

Less than two months after the couple were married, Bill departed for South Dakota. The discovery of gold in the Black Hills by Horatio Ross in 1874 had prompted a mad rush to the region, and nothing could keep Bill from his plan to travel there and find a rich claim of his own. Agnes chose to stay behind in Cincinnati. When she waved goodbye to her husband the day he left, she had no way of knowing it would be the last time she would see him alive.

On the afternoon of August 2, 1876, Hickok was engaged in a friendly game of poker in the Number 10 Saloon. Sometime during the game, Jack "Broken Nose" McCall, a former buffalo hunter, entered the saloon. No one paid attention to him until he pulled a .45-caliber six-shooter and shot Bill in the head. The bullet perforated the back of Bill's skull, exited the front, and lodged into the arm of the poker player sitting opposite Hickok. McCall fled the scene but was quickly apprehended.

Agnes was with her daughter in Ohio when she received news that Bill had been murdered. Bill Hickok was laid to rest in the Ingleside area of Deadwood, the site of the town's first cemetery, or Boot Hill, as graveyards were often called.

In April 1877, Agnes had a monument erected in Bill Hickok's memory at his gravesite at Mount Moriah's Cemetery in Deadwood. She returned to work, performing with the John Robinson Circus until the fall of 1880. Agnes lived with her daughter and her family in Ohio and moved with them to Jersey City, New Jersey, in 1883.

Agnes Lake Hickok died August 22, 1907, at the home of her daughter and son-in-law. According to the August 23, 1907, edition of the *New York Times*, Agnes died of "general debility." "She had been an invalid for ten years previous to her death." Agnes was eighty years old when she passed away and was buried in Cincinnati, Ohio, next to her first husband.

Herbert Hoover

d. 1964

A great American has ended a brilliant career of service to his fellow men. Above all, he was a humanitarian. He fed more people and saved more lives than any other man in history.

—Neil MacNeil, quoted in the obituary for his close friend Herbert Hoover, *New York Times*, October 21, 1964

When President Herbert Clark Hoover died on October 20, 1964, he had the longest retirement of any president. Born on August 10, 1874, in West Branch, Iowa, the future politician spent time as a gold miner in the Old West before making his way to the White House.

Herbert was one of three children born to Quakers Jessie and Huldah Hoover. Both of Herbert's parents had died by the time he was nine. His father had a heart attack, and his mother passed away after a bout with pneumonia. Herbert and his siblings were sent to Oregon to live with their uncle. Herbert attended Friends Pacific Academy in Newberg, Oregon, and from there went on to Stanford University in Palo Alto, California. He graduated in 1895 with a degree in geology. He struggled to find work as a surveyor and when nothing came along took a job mining gold at the Reward Gold Mine near Nevada City, California. He worked seventy hours a week digging and pushing ore carts. In 1896, he acquired a job as an assistant in a mine engineer's office in San Francisco.

A year later he secured a position as an engineer inspecting and evaluating mines for potential investors. Herbert then moved from the United States to Australia and then to China, where he worked as a mine engineer in both locations.

When Herbert came back to America in 1902, he continued in the engineering field touring various mines in Northern California and sharing what he knew about technology, management, and improving efficiency at mines such as the Empire Mine in Grass Valley, the richest hard rock mine in California. He became friends with the owner and manager of the Empire Mine, William Bowers Bourn and George Starr. The Bourns and Starrs loved to entertain and always invited mining engineers and stockholders to gatherings at their mansion near the Empire Mine. Herbert Hoover was a frequent guest.

In 1908, Hoover was recognized by the Mining and Metallurgy Association for his achievements in mine engineering. His interest in corporate finance turned his attention away from the physical aspect of mining toward the business side of the industry. Herbert formed his own company in London and invested in mining projects across England. His firm was profitable, and his reputation as a skilled entrepreneur grew rapidly.

When war broke out in Europe, the directors at the United States embassy called upon Herbert to help see to it that American tourists and expatriates stranded overseas could get back home. The successful endeavor caught the attention of the American ambassador, who solicited Herbert's help in organizing relief to starving citizens in countries such as Belgium.

When America entered the war in 1917, President Wilson called Herbert Hoover home to take charge of food organiza-

President Herbert Hoover LIBRARY OF
CONGRESS LC_USZ62-97849

tions in America. That was Hoover's initial foray into political office.

Hoover served as secretary of commerce and president of the American Child Health Organization; he was a leading member of the Red Cross before becoming the thirty-first president of the United States in 1928. He saw the country through the worst economic downturn in its history.

Try as he might, none of the plans President Hoover enacted helped to turn the Depression around for America. Neither drastic tax cuts, public works projects, nor reconstructing finance corporations brought about recovery. In his bid to serve a second term as president, he lost the 1932 election to Franklin Roosevelt.

Hoover was critical of FDR and his New Deal and made his opinion known in several books he wrote about his life in and out of office. He was vocal about all the presidents that followed after him and the work they did. He gave speeches condemning America's entry into World War II as well as the Korean and Vietnam Wars.

On October 20, 1964, President Hoover was at his home in New York City working on another book when he was stricken with a sudden and massive internal hemorrhage. He lapsed into a coma and could not be revived. He was buried at the Quaker Cemetery in West Branch, Iowa. Present at his graveside were his two sons and their families; Senator Barry Goldwater of Arizona, the Republican nominee for president; and representatives of President Lyndon Johnson and Harry S. Truman.

Herbert Clark Hoover, the onetime mining surveyor and engineer, was ninety years old when he passed away. He was remembered by his friends as someone who respected the westward trek and the last of the famous pioneers.

President Herbert Hoover's tombstone COURTESY HERBERT HOOVER PRESIDENTIAL LIBRARY-MUSEUM

Sarah Ann Horn

d. 1839

Indians took captives for several reasons. One reason was revenge.

—*The Indian Captivity Narrative 1500–1900*
by Katheryn Zebelle-Derounian-Stodola and James Arthur Levernie

In February 1838, Sarah Ann Horn was driven to Taos, New Mexico, in the wagon of two trackers and traders who had purchased her from a cruel miner living in the Sangre de Cristo Mountains in southern Colorado. The twenty-six-year-old English woman was thin and frail, and her clothes were ragged and torn. She had endured a harrowing adventure and was a broken and dispirited woman.

Sarah was a wife and mother of two boys when she and her husband moved from London to New York in 1833. From there the Horns signed on with a company bound for a settlement in Texas. The Horns and other colonists arrived at a place called Beales Settlement on the Rio Grande in the Spanish province of Texas in March 1834. The family tried for two years to make their homestead work. One poor crop after another, combined with continual attacks on fellow farmers and ranchers by Comanche

Indians and the progress of the Texas revolution, prompted their decision to leave the area and return to England.

The Horns were en route to Mexico to set sail for home when they were attacked by a large band of Comanche Indians. The Indians massacred Sarah's husband and the other men in the party traveling with them. Sarah, her sons, John and Joseph, and a Mrs. Harris were taken captive.

The Indians, some forty or fifty strong, left the area with their hostages in tow. Sarah and others were taken to an Indian camp deep in a thicket. According to her memoirs, upon arrival they "almost suffocated from the stench of rotten horse meat, which was lying around the lodges."

The white women and children were seated under guard on the ground. John and Joseph were stripped naked and left in that state. The Indians took the two women's bonnets, handkerchiefs, combs, and rings. When darkness fell, the Indians ate the stale horse meat lying about but offered their captives nothing, not even water. Before retiring, the raiding party bound Mrs. Harris, Sarah, and the two boys hand and foot.

The following morning the mules were saddled and the captives placed on the animals. Sometime after the Indians began their march, Sarah's mule bolted, throwing both her and John, riding with her, to the ground. She was unhurt, but the boy's shoulder was badly lacerated and bruised.

The captives were not fed until the third day of the journey. The Comanche Indians gave them all a little to eat before taking to the trail again. After their scarce morsels of food were devoured, the prisoners were placed back on the mules and led along the way. The Horn boys were left naked for the journey, and the hot sun cruelly blistered their bodies.

The Indians kept moving daily and Sarah learned that they were near Matamoros, Mexico. They came to a stream of water, and some of the warriors rode across. Sarah saw some American men on the opposite bank, and for a brief moment she was hopeful they might all be rescued. When she heard the report of many guns she knew the Indians had killed the white men and all her hopes were dashed.

When the Indians returned from killing the white men, they brought back with them a small, delicate-looking Spaniard. He had been stripped of most of his clothing. The Indians made him sit down, and then they quizzed him as to where his home was and how many were in his family. As soon as they obtained this information they returned his clothes and the entire company started for his home. That night they camped, and while the Spaniard slept, his captives shot him to death with arrows.

The next morning the Indians reached the dead man's house. They killed his wife and babies and plundered his home. Then they explored the creek bank nearby and discovered two Spaniards and an American living there. They dispatched them quickly and made camp at the scene of the murders.

Sarah's son John was now in agonizing pain from the injury to his shoulder. Finally an Indian took the child to the creek and covered the wound with mud. Miraculously, it began to heal.

The Indians resumed their wanderings. They crossed a large road and some of the warriors hid behind the trees. Soon a white man and his servant rode by, and the savages killed them. By now the captives were numb with constant pain and shock. It became a matter of routine to expect fresh atrocities. They lost track of the days as well as the attacks on those who passed them, and wondered only that they were still alive.

The Indians' constant wandering led them back to the spot where the Horn party had been attacked. It was now two weeks from the date of the massacre, the women surmised, but the bodies of the slain men still lay on the ground nude and scalped, deterioration quite advanced.

After a short stay, the Indians resumed their travels and rode to the spot where they had murdered the Spaniard. There the

Indians separated into three companies. Sarah, her sons, and Mrs. Harris were no longer together.

The Indians who held Sarah and her sons continued on the move until mid-June. Joseph slipped off his mule one day while crossing a stream, and the Indians refused to help him. They wouldn't allow Sarah to go to his rescue either. She raged at the warriors for their cruelty. Finally, Joseph was able to make his way to the bank of the stream. The Indians forced him to walk the balance of the day.

After several more days of travel, the Indians returned to their lodges in the thicket, and the three companies came together, Sarah and Mrs. Harris meeting again.

Mrs. Harris seemed barely alive. After a short stay the Indians moved again, and yet again they separated into three companies, each moving in a different direction. This time the Horn children were separated from their mother.

The company with whom Sara was traveling came to a group of lodges and she was taken to the family of the Indian who claimed her as his prisoner as he had been the first to lay hands on her at the time of the massacre. The squaw who became her mistress was exceptionally cruel to her. Often the squaw would fly into a rage and throw anything at hand at Sarah. Sarah was put to work dressing buffalo hides and doing other labor-intensive chores around the camp. She was fed regularly for her efforts. Mrs. Harris was also made to do chores, but the family that had taken her in would beat her and deprive her of food. She often came to Sarah to beg for scraps of something to eat.

Sarah had been separated from her boys for two months when two little Spanish boys who were also captives came to her and told her that a white boy had just arrived a short distance away. They asked if he was her son. Sarah obtained permission to go to him and found the child to indeed be Joseph. All his hair but a small tuft had been shorn. He was covered with black and red paint. He had been adopted into the tribe. Sarah was allowed to be with him for only a short time.

Since the Indians were again on the move, it wasn't until four months later that Sarah had any news of her son John. The Indians came together to hunt buffalo, and the party who held John came to Sarah's lodge. She was allowed to visit him for three hours.

The time dragged until 1837 replaced 1836. One day Sarah learned that they were near the borders of the Spanish Province of New Mexico. There the Indians waylaid and killed five Spaniards.

A short time later some white men came to the Comanche camp and tried to buy Sarah and Mrs. Harris, but the Indians refused. They were permitted to give the women clothing and carry food to the Horn children, but were then sent on their way. In the latter part of June 1837, some traders from Santa Fe succeeded in buying Mrs. Harris from the Indians.

The Indians began to move again, and Sarah was on the trail with them for three months. It was now September 1837, and they were near San Miguel, in the Province of New Mexico. Sarah was advised that she was to be sold to the Spaniards when they reached the settlement.

A few days later she was painted, put astride a mule, and taken to San Miguel. A wealthy land and business owner offered to buy her for two horses, but his bid was refused. After several days passed, he approached the Indians again. This time he offered them a horse, four bridles, two blankets, two mirrors, two knives, tobacco, and some powder and balls. The Comanche relented. After a year or more of horrible slavery, Sarah was free! Or so she thought.

Sarah was led to the home of a businessman who owned a livery and a mercantile. She was treated little better than a servant there, not even allowed to eat at the family table. She was put to work making linen shirts to sell at the store. Sarah was traded to an American miner in late 1837. In early 1838 she decided to travel with a party of American traders to the United States. She had delayed her departure because she still hoped desperately that she might recover her children.

In February 1838, two men by the name of Workman and Rowland of Taos sent Sarah two dresses and requested that she delay her departure until they made one more effort to buy her children from the Indians. They asked her to come to Taos. In March Sarah arrived in Taos and spent the time equally with the Workmans and Rowlands.

Workman and Rowland sent men out to the Comanche authorizing them to buy the Horn children at any price. The men returned empty handed. They informed Sarah that Joseph had died from starvation and exposure to the elements. An appeal was made to the United States government for aid in recovering John. Since the Comanche in New Mexico and Texas were not within the jurisdiction of the government, her plea was refused. However, she was referred to the Republic of Texas, but that country had too many problems to undertake a rescue.

With all hope of recovering her children gone, Sarah left for the United States in August 1838, the only woman in a large caravan. The party reached Independence, Missouri, safely in November 1838. Sarah was received into the home of David Workman, brother of the William Workman with whom she had stayed in Taos. She remained there writing a narrative of her horrible captivity with the Comanche. Her objective in writing the book was to obtain funds with which to return to her native England.

Mrs. Harris returned to her family in Boonsville, Missouri, after her liberation. Still young, she died soon after reaching that city. The cause of death was the exposure and abuse she had received at the hands of the Indians.

What became of Sarah's son John is not known. He was not returned to his mother during her lifetime. Still afflicted with injuries sustained during her captivity, Sarah died in 1839 in Pulaski County, Missouri. In 1851, a shortened version of her narrative was published in Cincinnati.

Lozen

d. 1890

Among Geronimo's band of thirty-six loyal warriors was an unassuming medicine woman named Lozen. The petite, plain woman dressed like the braves with whom she fought, and the courageous renegade who led the group would not make a move without her wise counsel. Geronimo believed that her divine power kept him and his followers out of harm's way for so long. Without her ability to detect the enemy's nearing presence, the Apache would have perished.

From 1882 to 1886, Geronimo's desperate band of braves eluded US Army scouts. The few Natives were the last of the

Lozen, top row, center NATIONAL ANTHROPOLOGICAL ARCHIVES, SMITHSONIAN INSTITU-
TION [2517-A]

free Apache, stubborn holdouts who refused to surrender, be
forced from their land, and placed on a reservation. Many Apache
believed it was better to die like a warrior than to live like dogs off
the scraps from emigrants they referred to as "white eyes." Lozen
honored the beliefs of her people and used her gift to keep the
white eyes at bay.

Lozen believed the god Ussen, who created all parts of the
earth, gave her the power to foresee danger. She would stand qui-
etly with her arms outstretched and her hands slightly cupped; she
would listen to the wind and sniff the air. Somehow she knew if
danger was near.

Lozen was born a member of the Mimbres tribe of Apache
in 1827. Her family lived near Ojo Caliente in New Mexico. Her
father was a leading member of his band, and her mother was a

well-respected woman. Not unlike most Indian children at the time, Lozen learned to ride a horse when she was very young. By the age of eight, she was considered an expert rider. From early on it was clear to her parents that she would not assume the traditional female role. She loved hunting and playing rough games with her brother, Victorio, and the other boys in the tribe. Her skill with a bow and arrow and a sling were exceptional. Like her father and his father before him, she was a born warrior.

Lozen's homeland, a stretch of ground that encompassed parts of New Mexico, Arizona, and northern Mexico, was rich with gold. The Mexicans were the first to invade the territory and try to possess the precious metal. They came by the hundreds, feverishly digging into the earth like coyotes. When they tired of searching for the nuggets themselves, they made slaves out of some of the Cheyenne and Apache in the area. Indian leaders quickly formed raiding parties in an effort to take back the land the Mexicans occupied and to free the Native slaves. Among them was Mangas Colorados, chief of the Membreno Chiricahua, as well as Cochise, Geronimo, and, in time, Lozen's brother, Victorio. Each pledged to resist the colonization of his native soil by the Spaniards and the incursion of white fortune-seekers on their way to California.

Lozen's young eyes witnessed numerous battles and countless brutal deaths. Often Apache were slaughtered during so-called peace negotiations between Indian council members and the gold seekers. Apache sought revenge for every life that was taken at the hand of their enemies. Mexican prisoners were occasionally taken and would be led out bound and gagged before the tribe. Then the wives, daughters, and mothers of the murdered Apache would kill the men. Lozen watched them cut the miners into pieces with knives or crush their skulls under the weight of their horses. Eventually the harsh retaliation forced the Mexicans to abandon the area and retreat south. Troubles for the Apache, however, were far from over. They were warned by other tribes that the white eyes were coming and were like the leaves on the trees—too numerous to count.

Before the white eyes overtook their land and many Native traditions were abandoned, Lozen would learn about the remarkable Apache women who had gone before her. They were shamans and warriors, mothers and hunters—women she admired and longed to be like. Shortly after her coming-of-age ceremony was celebrated by the tribe, Lozen journeyed to the sacred mountain to ask her god for a gift to help her people. It was a ritual all Indian women went through. While at the sacred mountain, she was given the power to understand horses and the ability to hear and see the enemy. If an enemy was near, she would feel his presence in the heat of her palms when she faced the direction from which he would come. She could determine the distance of the enemy by the intensity of the heat. The Apache sorely needed a woman with Lozen's unique talent; they didn't have enough warriors or enough power to battle the overwhelming white invaders.

Among the important influences in Lozen's life was her older brother, Victorio. From boyhood he had been groomed to be chief of the Chiricahua Apache tribe. He was blessed with the power of war and the handling of men. Tall and imposing, he was respected by all members of the band and referred to by other leaders as the perfect warrior. Lozen rode with Victorio and served as his apprentice. The two combined their powers and led warriors on many successful raids against white prospectors who attacked peaceful Apache camps. Nothing they did could stem the tide of settlers entering their country.

The ground covering the western territories was soaked with the blood of Natives and ambitious pioneers alike. The US government sent soldiers to the Southwest and built army posts where needed to give settlers protection along the Santa Fe Trail. Presidents Ulysses S. Grant and Rutherford B. Hayes sent envoys to the various Indian nations to negotiate peace and prevent further war. Lozen and Victorio attended those meetings, but were wary of the promises made by the white leaders. In time the US government broke all agreements made with the Apache and forced Lozen and the other Chiricahua onto the Warm Springs Apache Reservation in San Carlos, Arizona.

San Carlos was a hellishly hot, desert land, and the Chiricahua were unable to grow crops there as they had when they resided in the Mimbres Mountains. They could not provide for themselves and had to depend on the government for food and supplies. Between the hungry tribe and provisions, however, stood the corrupt government agents working at the reservation, who were stealing funds meant for Indians to purchase food.

Victorio appealed to General John Howard, an Indian agent overseeing the Apache's transition from plains living to the reservation, and requested that his people be returned to their homeland. Howard agreed to take the matter to President Grant. Lozen waited by her brother's side for word from the government. Two years passed before the appeal was officially granted.

The Apache's time in Ojo Caliente was short lived. Government rations set aside for the tribe were diverted again, and, when the Natives began stealing from the settlers, the army quickly rounded them up and marched them back to San Carlos. Conditions at the Warm Springs Reservation had not improved since they'd last been there. Not only was the lack of supplies still a problem, but outbreaks of malaria and smallpox were now claiming the lives of hundreds of Chiricahua. Victorio called together the Apache leaders for a council meeting. Lozen was the only woman allowed to attend.

After much discussion Victorio and Geronimo decided to leave the reservation, taking with them all who wanted to return to New Mexico. On September 2, 1877, a band of 320 Apache fled Warm Springs. Lozen was among them.

Lozen and Victorio raided camps as they traveled. They killed herders, mules, and steers, stopping only long enough to cut up the animal meat. Lozen's powers protected the band from the enemy's fast approach. Soldiers eventually overtook the group and tried to persuade them to return to the reservation. The brother and sister team was warned that any Indian found off the reservation would be killed.

"We'll not be killed; we'll be free," Lozen replied. "What is life if we are imprisoned like cattle in a corral?"

Lozen's words inspired her brother. Victorio vowed to stay and fight to return to his homeland. A warrant was quickly issued for his arrest. The Apache waged war against troops who tried to bring their chief to justice. The desperate band stayed alive and thwarted army capture by stealing food and horses. They ran from and fought off both American and Mexican soldiers, and survived on the run for three years at various spots in Texas, Arizona, New Mexico, and Mexico.

In mid-October 1880, Lozen and Victorio were separated while trying to flee from US Army troops. When she met up with her tribe at the reservation in Mescalero she learned that her brother had been killed by Mexican soldiers near Tres Castillos Mountains. Victorio and his band of loyal followers were riding hard into Mexican territory, hoping to lead US troops away from the mountains and onto the plains. The Indians were ambushed by the Mexican soldiers. Lozen was heartsick, convinced that had she been with Victorio the group never would have been surprised.

Lozen would never be the same. Inspired by her brother's drive to spare his people the ignominy of imprisonment and slavery, Lozen, along with the remaining Natives, prepared to do the only thing they knew: to fight and die as warriors. After several months battling with Mexican and US soldiers, the handful of warriors, their wives, and their children returned to the San Carlos Reservation. At San Carlos the band could rest, accumulate food and supplies, and recruit more warriors.

Lozen and the dedicated tribesmen who wanted to live again on their own land joined forces with Geronimo, then left the reservation and headed south toward the Sierra Madre. As the party traveled, Geronimo consulted Lozen's powers just as Victorio had done. The band raided sheep and cattle ranches for sustenance while on the run. Geronimo devised a plan of attack on forty men serving as cavalry police and scouts. With those men out of the way, Geronimo determined he could move about Apache land undetected. A plan was also set to destroy telegraph wires so communication between army posts would be minimized. One by one the scouts and police fell at the hands of Geronimo's warriors.

Geronimo relied greatly on Lozen to keep his braves from danger. Without her help the Apache would not have met their objective. For a while the Natives were happily camped in the Chiricahua Mountains, but more settlers were pouring into the wilderness, and for their safety the government would not allow the determined Apache to continue their actions. Over time the Mexican and US troops managed to track and capture a number of renegade Apache until only thirty-six were left on the run. Lozen and Geronimo were among them.

In August 1886, the Chiricahua tribe was backed against the wall. With so few members left to take up the cause of freedom, and the lack of food and supplies taking its toll on the last of the holdouts, Geronimo was faced with the decision to surrender to the white eyes. General Nelson A. Miles was sent to negotiate Geronimo's surrender. He was hesitant at first, but Lozen convinced him to sit down and talk with the soldiers.

Geronimo listened to the military leaders and agreed to stop fighting if they could all return to the reservation and live at Turkey Creek, New Mexico, on farms. General Miles explained that he could only deliver the message to his superior officers and added that this was their last chance to surrender. Geronimo reluctantly agreed to lay down arms.

In retaliation for the Chiricahua Apache's success at resisting imprisonment, the entire tribe—more than five hundred people, most of whom were living on the San Carlos Reservation—was deported from Arizona. Lozen was among the leaders shipped by train from Fort Bowie, Arizona, to Fort Pickens, Florida. US soldiers placed all the Indians in two cars, packing them in like cattle. Many died en route to the coast. Even more succumbed once they reached Florida. Pneumonia, meningitis, and malaria claimed the lives of hundreds of men, women, and children. Army post doctors also reported deaths due to depression at the conditions.

Lozen never saw her homeland again. She fell victim to tuberculosis and died in late 1890. She was buried in an unmarked grave.

Asa Mercer

d. 1917

*I appeal to high-minded women to go into the West to
aid in throwing around those who have gone before the
restraints of well-regulated society; to cultivate the higher
and purer facilities of man by casting about him those
refining influences that true women always carry with
them; to build up happy homes, and let true sunlight shine
round the hearthstone.*

—LETTER BY ASA MERCER,
NEW YORK TIMES, SEPTEMBER 30, 1865

When pioneer and businessman Asa Mercer died on August 10,
1917, in Buffalo, Wyoming, few in the ranching community
recalled the plan he devised to remedy the lack of single women in
the Northwest in the 1860s.

It began with an ad placed on February 24, 1860, that testi-
fied to the serious shortage of a desired commodity in Washington
Territory.

*Attention Bachelors: Believing that our only chance for
the realization of the benefits and early attainments of
matrimonial alliances depends on the arrival in our*

midst of a number of the fair sex from the Atlantic States, and that, to bring about such an arrival a united effort and action are called for on our part, we respectfully request a full attendance of all eligible and sincerely desirous bachelors of this community assemble on Tuesday evening next February 28, in Delim and Shorey's building, to devise ways and means to secure this much-needed and desirable emigration to our shores..

Signed by nine leading citizens, the advertisement was picked up by other newspapers and reprinted across the country. They had hopes of attracting industrious, young women to the rich and rugged Northwest, where a few thousand men were working on making fortunes in timber, fishing, farming, and other endeavors. There were a few favorable responses to the announcement but no solid plan was in place to import the desired commodity to the area.

By 1860, the pioneers in Washington Territory had established thriving communities along Puget Sound and were busy carving out farms and ranches along the coast and toward the foothills of the Cascades. The temperate climate, rich fisheries, and timber resources proved the raw material upon which to build a comfortable life. The prosperous and clean-living young men populating the region in 1858 were "eager to put their necks in the matrimonial noose."

In 1860, Asa Shinn Mercer hit upon a scheme to take the next step in the recruitment effort. He would import bachelorettes by traveling to the East Coast, where women were in abundance, and actively promoting the unequaled advantages of Washington Territory. That idea and its sequel were part of the fascinating career of A. S. Mercer, who found his own bride among those he recruited for Washington Territory.

Fresh from college when he followed his older brother, popular Seattle pioneer Judge Thomas Mercer, to the Northwest, Asa slipped right into place in the ambitious new town. Asa worked

Asa Mercer MUSEUM OF HISTORY AND INDUSTRY, SEATTLE

enthusiastically to help erect a college, and he became a teacher at the Territorial University when it opened in 1861. He also served as the unofficial acting president when the first man recruited turned down the job, and he helped to recruit new students who could afford to pay the fees, which became part of his compensation.

The lack of marriageable women had become a serious detriment to progress. What good was a university if there were no wives to produce the sons to populate its halls? Seeing an unfilled need, Asa rushed to the rescue. He solicited private contributions to make a trip to the East Coast and raised enough money to go to New England in 1863, hoping to bring back several hundred suitable ladies.

Asa wanted to attract hundreds of people, primarily marriageable women, but he was doomed to disappointment. As a result of all his efforts, only eleven unattached women paid $225 for passage and boarded the SS *Illinois* when it headed out to sea in the spring of 1864 on that "maiden voyage." The women were welcomed to Seattle, and all but two found husbands. Lizzie Ordway, who never married, was devoted to teaching and eventually became a country school superintendent. Another of the young ladies died, apparently of heart trouble.

Capitalizing on the buzz generated by his success, small though it was, Asa ran for a seat on the territory's governing council. He won the seat and served in the Territorial Legislative Assembly through January 1865. Then he undertook another recruiting expedition to the East.

A few months after arriving, Asa sent a letter from Lowell, Massachusetts, to the folks back home. It was printed in the *Seattle Gazette* and announced: "The 19th of August I sail from New York with upwards of three hundred war orphans—daughters of those brave, heroic sons of liberty, whose lives were given as offerings to appease the angry god of battle on many a plain and field in our recent war to perpetuate freedom and her institutions."

Asa asked the citizens of Seattle to prepare to house and care for the young ladies. He vouched for their intelligence and moral character. The paper reprinted his letter, and communities immediately appointed welcoming committees, though some were dismayed at how few women were headed for the shores.

While the welcoming committees back home were meeting, Asa was running into rough waters. The *New York Times* endorsed the plan to ship widows and orphans to the new territory, and that sent would-be emigrants to Asa's door. Opponents sounded dire warnings that Asa was a procurer for the dens of iniquity of the West and cautioned that those who left the safety of their families and their communities would suffer unmentionable fates.

While the newspapers capitalized on the sensational aspects of the plan, Asa's capital was shrinking at an alarming rate. As Seattle historian Clarence Bagley later reported, "He was ever prone to take whatever he urgently hoped for as certain of accomplishment. Asa's urgently-hoped-for voyage with hundreds of accomplished young women and families, however, was almost stopped on the docks of New York."

The ship that Asa said was to have been made available by the federal government ended up in the hands of another schemer who demanded a large sum to carry each of the passengers. The money Asa had been given by young bachelors to cover costs of bringing back wives was long gone. Funds provided by others to be used for various instruments had also been spent.

The delays, the loss of the ship, and finally the negative publicity caused many of the young ladies and their families to cancel plans to join the expedition. Five months late and several hundred ladies short, the SS *Continental* steamed out of New York Harbor on January 16, 1866. It arrived in San Francisco Bay on April 24, 1866. Some of the passengers, apparently daunted by dismal descriptions of the Pacific Northwest, decided to stay in sunny California.

The Mercer Maids, as they came to be called, found husbands and jobs in Washington, Oregon, and California. Only a few returned to the eastern seaboard.

Asa, with Annie, his Irish bride, whom he found among the maidens on the voyage, embarked on a series of promotional and career adventures that sent them from place to place all over the West. He authored a forty-page pamphlet, *The Washington Territory: The Great Northwest, Her Material Resources and Claims to Emigration*, which was the first of many tracts promoting the Northwest. Relocating to Oregon, he became a customs collector in Astoria, where he was accused of smuggling. The matter was eventually discharged following unsuccessful attempts to prosecute the case. He then became involved in shipping and real estate. It was in Oregon that he again displayed his knack for promotion and began writing for newspapers.

By the 1880s, Asa, his wife, and their children were living in Texas, where he founded and edited several publications. Moving to Wyoming, he started the *Northwestern Livestock Journal* and was involved with the Wyoming Stock Growers Association.

Annie died in 1900. She had given birth to eight children, three of whom died in infancy and one as a teenager. She had followed her husband wherever he went, never complaining publicly about his enthusiastic promotions and the failure and public criticism that seemed to follow almost everything he did. When he was seventy-eight years old, Asa died at his home in the Big Horn Mountains in 1917 and is buried at the Hyattville Cemetery at Hyattville, Wyoming. Though his schemes and dreams may have been bigger than the means to properly carry them out, his activities add a richly colored thread to the tapestry of western history.

Annie McIntyre Morrow

d. 1934

Dedicated to the gritty resolve and courage of Annie Morrow, AKA "Peg Leg Annie," and her friend "Dutch Em."... their colorful spirit lives on in our hearts and minds through the stories, myths and truth, still told about these pioneer women.

—FROM A MEMORIAL PLAQUE ERECTED BY THE ATLANTA ARTS SOCIETY AT JAMES CREEK SUMMIT PASS

Her name was Annie McIntyre Morrow, and the story of her life and times in the Idaho mining camps of Atlanta and Rocky Bar is one of tragedy, courage, and resourcefulness. She was born in Van Buren County, Idaho, on September 13, 1858. Her mother died giving birth to her. Annie's father, Steve McIntyre, brought her to the mining camp of Rocky Bar in 1864, and the two settled there.

When Annie was six years old, her father became partners with George W. Jackson, owner of one of the richest gold mines in the vicinity, the Gold Star. The two men quarreled; there was a shoot-out, and McIntyre was killed, leaving Annie an orphan.

At the age of fourteen, Annie met a man named Morrow, and the two became romantically involved. They married in 1876,

Annie McIntyre Morrow IDAHO STATE
HISTORICAL SOCIETY #81-18-1

but the marriage was not a happy one because Morrow beat his young bride. Annie left Rocky Bar with her husband but returned a few years later without him. Whether her husband died or whether she left him is not known.

Not long after her return to the South Boise mining area, Annie began operating a boarding house in Atlanta, Idaho, fourteen miles from Rocky Bar. Annie was an angel of mercy in the mining camp. She never turned down a hungry man or one without money. Her boarding house was a haven to those who were down on their luck.

Annie's best friend was a German woman, Emma Van Losch, known in the mining camp as Dutch Em. The two shared a fondness for alcohol and were often seen going from one saloon to another sampling the various products. In mid-May 1898, Annie and Dutch Em started drinking, and by late evening the two were near drunk. In spite of a snowstorm raging outside, the pair decided to walk to Rocky Bar to attend a dance. They were not adequately clothed when they set out on their way, but they did take more to drink with them when they left.

The trail the two embarked on between Atlanta and Rocky Bar lay around Bald Mountain, a height of more than seven thousand feet. At daybreak a mail carrier from Atlanta was making his way up the summit to exchange mail with another carrier from Rocky Bar. The carrier reported passing the two women on the way up. A mountain blizzard swept down before he made his descent, and he failed to see them in the thick curtain of snow that engulfed the whole mountainside.

The raging blizzard lasted for two days, and everyone in the two mining camps of Atlanta and Rocky Bar were worried about Dutch Em and Annie. The third day after their departure, when the mail packer, Jackson, went on his run, he began a search for the two women. Three feet of fresh snow had fallen during the storm, and all the bushes and trees were covered with a mantle of white. Finally, in a deep canyon on the Atlanta side of the mountain, the mailman came upon Annie crawling about in the snow, jabbering in delirium. Her feet were frozen. Jackson carried her back to Atlanta and sent for Dr. M. J. Newkirk in Mountain Home, eighty miles away.

For five days Annie waited for the doctor. She drank whisky to kill the intense pain she was suffering from her frozen feet. Tate had made the mistake of building a fire in her room, and as Annie's feet thawed, her agony was almost unendurable. As she had no family, the miners took up a collection and hired a nurse to take care of her.

During the five days it took the doctor to reach Annie, various people of the camp suggested remedies to alleviate Annie's suffering. Annie's nurse even tried poultices of grated potatoes. The entire camp was sympathetic and tried to help in every possible way. When Dr. Newkirk finally arrived, gangrene had set in. He placed Annie on the kitchen table, gave her an anesthetic, and amputated both legs just below the knees.

After a time Annie's delirium left her, and she was able to relate her experiences on the tragic trip across the blizzard-held mountain. Search parties were dispatched to Bald Mountain to locate Dutch Em, and her frozen body was found about a mile from where Annie had been rescued. The men who found her saw that she was covered with Annie's underclothes.

Annie said that she was sure that she could have made it to safety after the blizzard struck, but she would not desert Em, who collapsed. The two women found a huge boulder and huddled against it. Annie tried to build a fire, but the snow had wet her matches, so the two lay close together in an effort to keep from freezing. Annie removed her underclothes and covered Em, but after twenty-four hours she froze to death. Annie couldn't remember anything beyond that.

After her legs healed, Annie made woolen pads for her stumps and started doing laundry for the miners of Rocky Bar. She worked hard and saved her money. She believed her life had changed for the better when she met and fell in love with a drifter named Henry Longheme. He convinced Annie to take her savings of twenty years, some $12,000, and give it to him to deposit in a bank in San Francisco. A month after he left the area, Annie received a letter from Henry. He was in New York and he wrote to let her know he was leaving the country. She never heard from him again, nor did she ever get back any of her money. She inquired of the bank in San Francisco and learned that her money had never been deposited there.

For a short time after Prohibition came into effect, Annie bootlegged in a little cabin near Rocky Bar. Toward the last years of her life, she was completely broke. The tenderhearted miners brought her groceries and carried wood to her cabin. Annie eventually developed cancer and died from the disease in 1934. She was seventy-six years old. She is buried in the Morris Hill cemetery in Boise.

George Parrott

d. 1881

Dr. John E. Osborne, early-day Wyoming governor . . .
went west from Vermont. "Big Nose" George Parrot was
lynched by a Wyoming posse. Dr. Osborne . . . removed
a square of skin from the body and had it tanned and
fashioned into a pair of shoes.

—Essex County Republican,
May 7, 1943

George Lathrope, better known as Big Nose George Parrott, was perhaps the most notorious bandit in Wyoming in the 1870s. At one time or another he appeared in all of the Rocky Mountain States at the head of his hard-bitten gang of mail robbers and murderers.

Fearless and brutal, "Big Nose" George staged many a successful mail robbery along the tracks of the Union Pacific strung through the Wyoming desert, but like most of the other bad men of his time he tried one job too many and paid for his career in crime.

It was mid-August 1878 when Parrott and his men decided to rob the United Pacific train a short distance from the little mining town of Carbon, Wyoming. They used the same trick Jesse

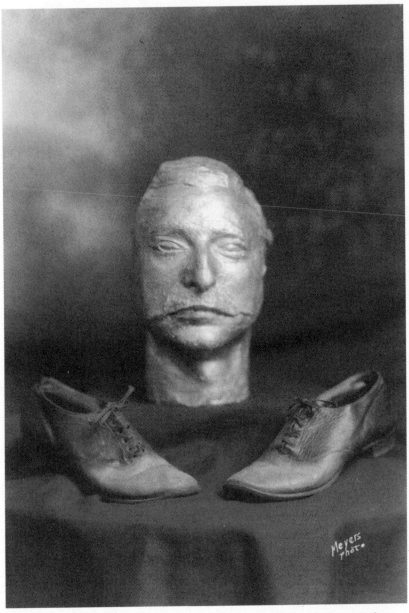

A plaster cast of "Big Nose" George Parrott's head and the shoes made from his skin. WYOMING STATE ARCHIVES, DEPARTMENT OF STATE PARKS AND CULTURAL RESOURCES

James had when he robbed a train at Adair, Iowa, in 1873. They pulled spikes on a downhill curve and a length of wire was attached to the rail. It was their intention to pull and spread the rail from their place of concealment and pitch the train down a ravine. Once the train had derailed, the plan was to rifle the pay-car and make for some desolate camp in the plains.

However, Parrott's scheme was doomed to failure as the loose rail was spotted by section foreman Eric Brown, who put two and two together and suspected the planned robbery. Luckily he was not spotted by the outlaws and hurried into Carbon, where the news was flashed to Rawlins, sixty miles away. A posse headed by Deputy Sheriff Robert Widdowfield and a railroad detective named Tip Vincent was soon on its way to the scene.

The outlaws soon realized that the train was late for some reason or another, so Parrott sent one of his men into Carbon to see if he could learn the reason for the delay. It was not long before the man returned and hurriedly told his chief that the train was in fact late because of a washout in the road, that their presence was known, and a posse was on its way.

"We have plenty of time before the posse from Rawlins gets here," Parrott told his men. "We'll just mosey to Elk Mountain and give them lawmen a surprise."

The outlaws rode to Rattlesnake Canyon near Elk Mountain and waited for the posse to put in an appearance. When it did, the outlaws ambushed them, killing Vincent and Widdowfield. It was August 19, 1878.

Parrott disappeared and turned up in a Butte saloon three weeks later. He drank too much and boasted of many of his escapades, including the unsuccessful attempt to rob a train at Carbon. A few days later he was arrested and given a hearing. He was sentenced to be hanged for first degree murder in April 1881 and thrown in jail in Rawlins, Wyoming.

Late in March 1881, he tried to escape the Carbon County jail by slugging jailer Rankin but failed to make good his escape. This act incensed the citizens of Rawlins to such a state, however, that they stormed the jail on the evening of March 22, 1881, and lynched the doomed man from a telegraph pole in the street.

To add a dash of horror to the morbid affair, Dr. John E. Osborne made a death mask of Parrott, also removing the skin from the dead outlaw's chest and fashioning it into a medicine bag. More of Parrott's skin got around. A tanned piece of it was in the possession of Professor Reed of Wyoming University at Laramie for many years. It finally found its way to E. E. Calvin, vice president of operations of the Union Pacific System and, incidentally, the man who took Parrott's confession.

The skin from both of Parrott's thighs was removed, tanned, and fashioned into a pair of shoes, which are currently in the possession of the Rawlins National Bank. The top of Parrott's skull was presented to Lillian Heath, Dr. Osborne's assistant, and she presented it to the Union Pacific.

On April 24, 1943, the eighty-nine-year-old Dr. Osborne, who had later served as governor of Wyoming, passed away, and the *Denver Post* carried an item about his activities in the Parrott matter.

Another article that appeared in the *Post* on March 12, 1950, told of the finding of the bones and base of the skull of Big Nose George in a barrel. They were uncovered while workmen were digging a foundation for a new store building in downtown Rawlins. A bottle of vegetable compound and a pair of shoes with glass nails were found with the bones.

Bass Reeves

d. 1910

*Bass Reeves was a unique character. Absolutely fearless
and knowing no master but duty, the placing of a writ in
his hands for service meant that the letter of the law would
be fulfilled though his life paid the penalty. . . . [He] faced
death a hundred times . . . with the simple faith that some
men have who believe that they are in the care of special
providence when they are doing right.*

—Muskogee Phoenix, January 15, 1910

News of the death of lawman Bass Reeves on January 12, 1910,
was posted in newspapers from Fort Smith, Arkansas, to Eufaula,
Oklahoma. Reeves was one of the first black Americans (if not the
first) to receive a commission as a deputy US marshal west of the
Mississippi River.

Born a slave in 1838, Reeves lived in Paris, Texas, for a number of years before fleeing slavery to live among the Indians in what
is now Oklahoma. He was a giant of a man, standing over six feet
tall. His look was made all the more imposing because of the black
hat he wore that was upturned in the front. He was an expert with
the twin Colts he wore on his hips and never backed down from

Bass Reeves RESEARCH DIVISION OF THE OKLAHOMA HISTORICAL SOCIETY

a challenge. According to the January 2, 1907, edition of the *Daily Ardmoreite*, Reeves was known as a "terror to the black outlaws and bootleggers." He had a reputation for never failing to capture a man he went after, bringing him in dead or alive.

A career in law enforcement was not Reeves's initial plan. In 1863 he bought land near Van Buren, Arkansas, with the intent to farm. Shortly after that, he married Nellie Johnson, and they immediately started a family. The idea that Reeves might not be entirely content with life as farmer and father came about when US Marshal James Fagan suggested Judge Isaac Parker hire him to be a marshal.

The Indian Territory was being overrun with thieves and murderers, and lawmen were needed to police the area and keep it safe. Reeves was an expert on the terrain and could speak several Native American languages. Reeves served for thirty-five years as a deputy US marshal. He covered seventy-five thousand square miles and captured more than three thousand criminals, killing fourteen.

Reeves was handy with a disguise should the situation call for it. On one occasion he dressed as a down-and-out hobo in search of food and shelter in order to arrest three known highwaymen. Pretending to be on the run from the law himself, Reeves traveled to the home of the bandits and talked his way inside. The unassuming men were arrested for their crimes and Reeves then marched them twenty-eight miles to jail. The outlaws were locked up and Reeves collected the $5,000 reward on the culprits.

Throughout his long and accomplished career, Reeves tracked down a number of ruthless criminals, such as cattle rustler Tom Story and bank robber Bob Dozier, but no desperado proved to be as difficult for Reeves to apprehend as his own son. In a violent rage, Reeves's oldest son, Benjamin, beat his wife to death. The young Reeves then fled to Indian Territory. Two weeks after receiving the arrest warrant, Bass returned with his son in tow. Benjamin was tried for murder, found guilty, and sentenced to life in prison at Fort Leavenworth, Kansas.

On November 11, 1909, the *Muskogee Times Democrat* reported that the seasoned law enforcement agent had become seriously ill at his home and that doctors did not expect him to live. He died on January 12, 1910. His funeral was one of largest seen in Muskogee. Hundreds of friends were in attendance: black, white, and Indian. Historians speculate Reeves was laid to rest in the Old Union Agency Cemetery in Muskogee, Oklahoma, but no one knows for certain where his body was buried. He was seventy-two years old when he died.

Kate Rockwell

d. 1957

No meeting of sourdoughs throughout the Pacific North-
west was complete without her and she filled the hours
with reminiscences of the days of the 1900 gold rush into
the Yukon Territory.
—LETHBRIDGE HERALD, FEBRUARY 22, 1957

A frigid wind blew hard past the weather-beaten exterior of the
Palace Garden Theatre in Dawson City, Alaska. It was the spring
of 1900, and gleeful patrons were tucked warmly inside, waiting
for the "Flame of the Yukon" to take the stage.

A fiery, red-headed beauty glided out before the crowd, her
violet eyes smiling. The men went wild with applause. The music
began, and the entertainer swayed with the beat, placing a gloved
hand to her breast and a fingertip to her lips and then, stretching
her arm out, beckoning her admirers. The elaborate red-sequin
dress she was wearing was form-fitting, and the long black cape
that draped over her shoulders clung to her alabaster skin.

The piano player accelerated his playing, and Kate gyrated
gracefully in and out of the shadow of the colored lights that flick-
ered across the stage. After a moment, with a slight movement of
her hand, she dropped the cape off her shoulders and it fell to the

Kate Rockwell BARRETT WILLOUGHBY, ALASKA AND POLAR REGIONS ARCHIVES, RAS-MUSON LIBRARY, UNIVERSITY OF ALASKA FAIRBANKS

floor. The glittering diamonds and rhinestones around her neck sparkled and shined. Ever so seductively, she picked up a nearby cane adorned with several yards of red chiffon and began leaping, while twirling the fabric-covered walking stick. Around and around she fluttered, the chiffon trailing wildly about her like flames from a fire, the material finally settling over her outstretched body. The audience erupted in a thunderous ovation. She was showered with nuggets and pouches filled with gold dust. This dance would make her famous.

Kathleen Eloisa Rockwell came to the Klondike in April 1900. She attracted a following wherever she performed across Alaska. Kate was born in Junction City, Kansas, on October 4, 1876, to parents of Scotch-Irish descent. Her love for music and dancing began when she was a toddler. The piano and the button accordion had an intoxicating effect on her. Her wealthy stepfather provided the gifted child with the education she needed to hone her natural talents. She was trained in French, voice, and instrumental music at the Osage Mission in Kansas.

Kate's parents eventually moved to Spokane, Washington, leaving their daughter behind to complete her studies. She visited her family during the summer months, when Spokane was abuzz with entertainment opportunities. Inspired by performances by traveling troupes of vaudevillians who sang and danced their way across the Northwest, she dreamed about joining the troubadours and of someday being a New York stage actress.

Kate moved to New York with her parents in the late 1800s and found work as a chorus girl in one of the city's many theaters. She enjoyed her time on the stage and quickly became addicted to the nightlife of the big city. In time, Kate took her act on the road. She traveled across the Great Plains states, working her way back and forth across the country. She stood out among the other singers and dancers by always holding her head up high and smiling proudly for the appreciative audiences.

Kate returned to Washington when a girlfriend told her that dancers were needed at a theater in Spokane. An astute theater manager in town offered the entertainer a contract and reimbursed her for all travel expenses, but the theater where she signed to perform was nothing more than a minuscule stage in the back of a saloon. Kate was required to work the bar between acts for a percentage of the profits from the beer she sold. She threatened to leave right away, but the manager reminded her of the signed contract in his pocket. Kate had no choice but to stay.

Her pleasing personality and beautiful face helped sell a lot of beer. Soon Kate was rolling in money. Enticed by further financial gain, she ended up staying longer than she'd planned. Once the contract was up, Kate traveled to Seattle to perform at the People's Theatre.

Not long after she arrived in Seattle, the Savoy Theatre in British Columbia invited her to join its vaudeville troupe. She was promised great pay and the opportunity to introduce two new song-and-dance routines each week. This was the break for which she'd been waiting. She signed with the company, leaving the People's Theatre after only two weeks.

Then Kate came down with a serious case of gold fever. A gold rush had hit Alaska Territory, and Kate was eager to get in on the quest for riches. There was a demand for entertainers in the mining towns across the Yukon, and Kate believed she could earn a fortune filling that need. She sailed for Skagway, Alaska, aboard a crowded supply vessel with her singing and dancing partner, Gertie Jackson. The two had developed an act they were sure would attract large audiences.

The women found the conditions in Skagway less than hospitable. The streets were unpaved, buildings that housed businesses were little more than shacks, and crime was rampant. Gertie abandoned the act shortly after the duo found work. She hated Skagway and headed back for "civilization" aboard the next steamer.

Kate stayed in Alaska, determined to make her way across the territory to the mining camps where the richest gold strikes were being made. She earned money to continue her journey by working at saloons and makeshift theaters, perfecting her "buck and wing" (tap) dancing. She did an average of twenty shows a day and after a year and a half raised more than $20,000—enough money to fund her own string of theaters. Miners in Whitehorse, Alaska, were so captivated by her singing, dancing, and kindness to the down-and-out that they honored her by writing her name with Champagne corks on the ceiling of a hotel in town.

In the spring of 1900, the Savoy Theatre ensemble again invited Kate to join. The company was passing through Whitehorse on its way to a playhouse in Dawson and felt she would be the perfect addition to the show. The Savoy was the largest burlesque and musical troupe ever to invade the Klondike. It was made up predominantly of pretty girls who danced, sang, acted, juggled, and did magic tricks. The troupe was welcomed with great fanfare when it arrived in Dawson. The formerly empty theater was quickly transformed into the liveliest spot in town.

Kate won over the rowdy audiences of merchants, gamblers, and sourdoughs with her tearful ballads and quick-stepping dance moves, sealing her fame as "Klondike Kate." She had many suitors, but her heart settled on a waiter named Alexander Pantages who worked at the theater. Alexander was a handsome Greek man with thick, black hair. He was attentive to and protective of Kate, and she was captivated by his good looks and charming accent. He had come to Alaska seeking a fortune in gold.

Alexander dreamed of owning a chain of playhouses—a dream he had in common with Kate. She was the undisputed queen of the dance-hall girls and capable of making big money. He made plans to capitalize on her talents and affection for him.

The couple moved in together when Alexander was fired from the Savoy for skimping on the drinks. He promised to marry

Kate as soon as he found other employment. In the meantime, Kate supported Alexander in high fashion. Her act became even more popular, especially when she added a fast-paced roller-skating routine. She never failed to fill the Savoy with people and enchant her audience with throaty songs sung in tearful seriousness. Kate was earning more money than any other entertainer in Alaska.

She and Alexander opened a theater of their own, calling the place the Orpheum. Kate produced and directed her own stage show, and the Orpheum quickly became the hottest spot in Dawson. Within a couple of months, Alexander as manager and Kate as entertainer were bringing in $8,000 per week.

Alexander and Kate were a professional success, but their personal relationship began to falter. He had postponed their marriage several times, and Kate was growing impatient. He told Kate that he wanted to put off their wedding until they had acquired more theaters and attained a more comfortable lifestyle.

The pair took Kate's variety act to Nome (where more gold was being found) and then to San Francisco. They bought theaters in each location. They registered at various hotels as husband and wife. Finally, they decided to settle in Seattle. Alexander returned to Dawson to take care of their business affairs while Kate traveled to Washington alone.

While passing through Vancouver, British Columbia, Kate purchased a quaint nickelodeon that included a biograph machine for showing moving pictures. The new form of entertainment, along with her own vaudevillian act, appealed to patrons, and in no time the theater was turning a profit. At first Alexander was furious at Kate for buying the nickelodeon; he thought the biograph was a passing oddity. He changed his mind, however, when he saw how much money the business was making. He bought a second movie house in Seattle called the Crystal Theatre, beginning the largest, most memorable chain in American entertainment history.

In the fall of 1903, Alexander booked his star, Klondike Kate, at a theater in Texas. She was a huge hit. Alexander rewarded her hard work by sending a lovely, seventeen-year-old violinist named Lois Mendenhall he had discovered to share the variety show stage in Galveston with Kate.

Kate took the dark-eyed beauty under her wing, helping her with her act and looking out for her well-being. Little did Kate know the impact this young woman would have on her life.

After more than a year of performing in Texas, Kate returned to Seattle. Alexander had put the money she'd sent home to good use, expanding their business holdings to include theaters in Portland, Tacoma, and Spokane. While Kate was performing at a Spokane theater, she received the heartbreaking news that Alexander had married someone else—none other than young Lois Mendenhall.

Kate was devastated and temporarily gave up the stage. She sank into a deep depression, growing weak from lack of nourishment and sleep. She stopped caring about her appearance and started drinking heavily. One of Kate's friends from her chorus-girl days helped snap her out of her despair long enough to take Alexander to court.

On May 26, 1905, a little more than two months after the marriage, Kate filed a $25,000 breach-of-promise lawsuit against Alexander. Alexander denied that he'd ever known her. Kate's fans were outraged. A front page article in the *Seattle Times* carried the headline, "Uses Her Money, Then Jilts the Girl."

Once all the testimony was heard, the court dismissed the case against Alexander and rejected any financial claim Kate had. The judge ruled that there wasn't enough physical evidence to prove Alexander had consented to marry Kate or that he had used her money in his business. Kate left the courtroom a shattered and demoralized woman. She would never be the same again.

Almost a year after Kate was jilted, she returned to the stage, teaming up with comedian Arthur Searles. They performed skits and song-and-dance routines on the vaudeville circuit. Unfortunately, audiences were more interested in silent movies by this time. Kate was eventually forced to retire from show business, trading in the spotlight for a small farm in Bend, Oregon. She married twice; one union ended with her husband's death, and the other ended in divorce. She kept busy tending to her homestead, and she periodically traveled to Dawson and Seattle to visit family and friends.

While her entertainment career had stalled, Alexander's was reaching its peak. His chain of show-houses had spread all over the West. "Going to the Pantages" (Alexander's last name) was a common expression for going to the theater.

On February 21, 1957, Kate Rockwell died peacefully in her sleep. She was eighty years old. She was cremated and her ashes were scattered over the Central Oregon desert. Prominent magazines like *Time* and *Newsweek* ran articles about her passing. The *Bulletin* newspaper in Bend, Oregon, conceded that she would never be forgotten and predicted that her story would grow as memories of the Alaska Gold Rush faded into distant history.

Lillian Russell

d. 1922

Lillian Russell (Mrs. Alexander P. Moore), bright star of American comic opera for three decades and internationally known as a professional beauty who died at 2:20 o'clock this morning, had been ill several weeks following a shipboard accident while returning from Europe. Her death was unexpected, as her physicians two days ago announced she had passed the crisis and would recover.

—THE *CLINTON HERALD*, JUNE 6, 1922

It was not so much Lillian Russell's great dramatic ability or her clear, well-trained voice as it was her personality and physical beauty that made her the most famous musical comedy star of her day and acclaimed for more than a generation as "America's greatest beauty."

Born on December 4, 1861, in Clinton, Iowa, Helen Louise Leonard had the kind of beauty that stopped traffic from her earliest years. She had a voice that her mother, Cynthia Rowland Leonard, an ardent feminist, paid to have trained when her daughter was still in her teens. Helen Louise was educated at the Convent of the Sacred Heart in Chicago and attended finishing

Lillian Russell ANNENBERG RARE BOOK AND MANUSCRIPT LIBRARY, UNIVERSITY OF
PENNSYLVANIA

school at Park Institute. She took singing lessons and sang in the church choir at the Episcopal church.

Her parents separated when she was in her teens, and her mother took Helen Louise and moved to New York, where young Helen started training for the grand opera. She could sustain the highest notes with virtually no effort, and do it again and again without strain. Her voice coach, Dr. Leopold Damrosch, told her mother that with a few years of training, he could make her a diva to rival the best.

Years of training and rehearsals, with only bit parts and backup roles as an understudy, lay before her on the road to stardom in opera. Helen Louise joined the Park Theatre Company in Brooklyn. She was eighteen when she danced onstage for the first time in the chorus of *H.M.S. Pinafore*, a Gilbert and Sullivan operetta that went on to resounding success.

Before the run of *Pinafore* was over, Helen Louise had accepted a proposal of marriage from an admirer in the show. She married the company's musical director, Harry Graham, which marked the end of her appearance in the chorus. She withdrew from the company and settled into domestic life, but her time as a homemaker didn't last.

In late 1879, Helen Louise gave birth to a son. A nurse was hired to care for the baby so the actress could once again take up her career. Her paycheck made a big difference for the little family. Her much older husband was not happy with his wife being the breadwinner, however; he wanted her to stay home and take care of their child. But a woman raised to be independent is not easily swayed when fame and fortune call.

Then one day Helen Louise returned from the theater to find her baby desperately ill. Despite all attempts to treat the infant, he died in convulsions. Apparently, the inexperienced nurse had accidentally pierced his abdomen with a diaper pin. Harry accused his wife of neglect, and he divorced her in 1881.

Grieving over the death of her son, feeling betrayed by her husband's accusation, and devastated over the end of her marriage, Helen Louise concentrated on her career. Tony Pastor, legendary producer of musical comedy, heard her sing at the home of a friend and consequently offered her a job. Helen Louise liked the immediate success she'd already tasted in comic opera. At nineteen, with a statuesque figure, golden curls, skin like "roses and cream," and a soprano voice that could do everything with ease, she had found her first mentor in Tony Pastor.

Pastor's theater specialized in send-ups of popular plays like *The Pirates of Penzance*, produced by Pastor as *The Pie Rates of Penn-Yann*. The impresario thought Helen Louise Leonard too dowdy and provincial a name for a gorgeous blonde with a voice of an angel. In mid-1881, Pastor presented her as "Lillian Russell, the English Ballad Singer." She chose the two names from a list, later saying she liked the way the names began and ended with the same letter.

Pastor gave Lillian parts that accentuated her talents. She was a rousing success, so much so that Pastor feared she would be spoiled by adulation. Instead of continuing to build her reputation in New York, he sent her west with Willie Edouin's touring company. Edouin was an actor, dancer, director, and theater manager. As Lillian traveled by rail toward the Pacific Ocean, she learned to play poker and pinochle.

In San Francisco Lillian Russell became the toast of the town. The City by the Bay was bubbling over with brash enterprise, fueled by newly made fortunes dug from the golden hills. The troupe that played *Babes in the Wood* and *Fun in a Photograph Gallery* earned recognition in the newspapers. Audiences all over the world were soon asking for Lillian Russell to perform for them.

By October 1881, she was back playing at New York's Bijou Opera House, a somewhat seasoned twenty-year-old performer who had no trouble on stage but had not yet learned the business side of the entertainment industry.

In May 1884, she married again, and again it was to a musician, English composer Edward Solomon. The winter of the following year, Lillian and her husband welcomed a baby daughter into the world, and they named her Dorothy Lillian.

Reality slapped the face of the famous beauty once more. In England a woman named Jane Isaacs Solomon filed suit against her husband—for bigamy. Edward was arrested in England, and Lillian's hopes for a happy married life were shattered. She announced she would seek an annulment. Although she concealed the pain of Solomon's betrayal, the luster of America's Beauty was tarnished by scandal.

Lillian decided to make another tour of the American West, and this one turned out to be much more successful. She signed with the J. C. Duff Company and embarked on a long tour of cities along the Pacific Coast. At the end of two seasons on the road, Lillian was a bigger star than ever. As she entered her thirties, she herself was bigger than ever. The hourglass figure that had contributed to her fame now required the tight cinching of a strong corset. Lillian, who reportedly could eat a dozen ears of corn as an appetizer, fully enjoyed the offerings of the best restaurants. Knowing her beauty was a huge part of her success, she began to exercise religiously. She became a fanatical bicyclist, and her friend, millionaire railroad salesman Diamond Jim Brady, presented her with a gold-plated bicycle.

Always questioned about her beauty secrets, Lillian recommended vigorous exercise at a time when the myth of women as the "weaker sex" was accepted without question. Lillian's advice flew in the face of convention. "Bicycle riding to women usually means pedaling along, dismounting every five or ten minutes, but this will not do at all if you mean to reduce your weight," she warned. In addition, and to the horror of those who already considered bicycles for women a tool of the devil, Lillian advised against wearing a corset while exercising. "Every muscle must be unhampered," she insisted.

In 1894, Lillian wed singer John Haley Augustin Chatterton, who styled himself Signor Giovanni Perugini. Her actress friend Marie Dressler portrayed the tenor as a conceited buffoon who stooped to embarrassing Lillian onstage. After several months of discord, Lillian kicked him out.

In 1899, Lillian joined Weber and Fields Music Hall in New York, where she earned more than $1,200 a week. Until 1904, when Joe Weber and Lew Fields dissolved their partnership, she enjoyed a fizzy success in comic opera. *Lady Teazle*, a musical version of *The School for Scandal*, showcased her talents as an actress. Minor surgery on her throat had not helped her deteriorating voice, so she began playing exclusively comic roles. She covered thousands of miles in her private railroad car to modest success and finally returned to vaudeville with a popular reprise of some of her most famous songs.

Still beautiful, fiercely intelligent, and as opinionated as her mother ever had been, Lillian began writing a syndicated newspaper column, lectured on health and beauty and love, supported the vote for women, and put out a line of cosmetics called Lillian Russell's Own Preparation.

In 1912 she married Alexander Pollock Moore, owner of the *Pittsburgh Leader*. Moore was everything her musician husbands had not been, and his power in conservative politics matched her interests well. She recruited for the Marine Corps and supported war bond drives during the First World War, and afterward raised money for the American Legion.

She performed steadily from 1914 to 1922. In 1922 she campaigned vigorously for Warren G. Harding for president; as a result, in 1922 President Harding appointed her as a special investigator on immigration. During a tour of Europe in this capacity, she sustained a bad fall and, despite the injuries, turned in her report urging restrictions on immigration. On June 6, 1922, the famous American Beauty, the superstar of the "Gay Nineties," died at her Pittsburgh home of "cardiac exhaustion." Lillian Russell was sixty-one years old.

Ellen Clark Sargent

d. 1911

Mrs. Ellen Clark Sargent was a woman of great force when she believed herself in the right and nothing could change her.

—Oakland Tribune, July 22, 1911

The memory of Ellen Clark Sargent's arrival in Nevada City, California, stayed with her all her life. Long after she had left the Gold Country, she recalled: "It was on the evening of October 23, 1852, that I arrived in Nevada [City], accompanied by my husband. We had traveled by stage since the morning from Sacramento. Our road for the last eight or ten miles was through a forest of trees, mostly pines. The glory of the full moon was shining upon the beautiful hills and trees and everything seemed so quiet and restful that it made a deep impression on me, sentimental if not poetical, never to be forgotten."

In the newly formed state of California, shaped by men and women who had endured unbelievable hardships to cross the plains, Ellen saw an opportunity to gain something she passionately wanted: the right to vote. Despite defeat after defeat, she never gave up.

Ellen Clark fell in love with Aaron Augustus Sargent, a journalist and aspiring politician, in Newburyport, Massachusetts, when they were in their teens. Both taught Sunday school in the Methodist church. Upon their engagement, Aaron promised to devote his life to being a good husband and making their life a happy one. But several years passed before he had a chance to make good on that promise.

In 1847, Aaron left Ellen in Newburyport to go to Philadelphia, where he worked as a printer. His interest in politics intensified with the new friends he made. Aaron, an ardent opponent of slavery, closely followed arguments of free-soilers and antislavery forces.

He worked as a print compositor and as a newspaper writer. However, the trade paid poorly. With word of the gold strike in California, Aaron borrowed $125 from his uncle and sailed from Baltimore on February 3, 1849, leaving Ellen with a promise to return and make her his wife.

Aaron arrived in the gold camp called Nevada in the spring of 1849 and was moderately successful in his search for gold. He then became a partner with several others in the *Nevada Journal* newspaper. But with a promise to keep, Aaron obtained the help of a friend and built a small frame house near the corner of Broad and Bennett Streets, right in the center of town. In January 1852, he returned to Newburyport to claim his bride. Aaron and Ellen were married on March 15 and returned to Nevada City in October of that year.

Ellen Sargent had no notion of the home she would find, but she was agreeably surprised. She later wrote an account of her arrival in Nevada City: "My good husband had before my arrival provided for me a one-story house of four rooms including a good sized pantry where he had already stored a bag of flour, a couple of pumpkins and various other edibles ready for use, so that I was reminded by them of a part of the prayer of the minister who had

Ellen Clark Sargent COURTESY SEARLS HISTORIC LIBRARY

married us, seven months before, in faraway Massachusetts. He prayed that we might be blessed in basket and in store. It looked like we should be."

Ellen set up housekeeping in a town where the cost of every-thing was astonishing. Eggs sold for three dollars a dozen, chick-ens for five dollars apiece.

"It did not take long for thrifty housewives to make a very good sweet cake, corn bread, and pudding without eggs," she wrote. Canned chicken and turkey were substituted for fresh, and women making homes in the gold camps used dried apples as well as dried fish. Beans and salt pork were plentiful. Along with eggs and fresh meat, vegetables were in short supply, and very costly.

Despite the preponderance of saloons and the raw nature of the town, Ellen loved her little home. Her one frustration with the housekeeping was in sharing space with the other tenants of the house—the four-footed ones. The ceilings were covered in muslin, which easily betrayed the presence of large rats. "We did not like their hills and dales, or the coloring of their landscapes, but they were no less happy on that account, if we may judge by the oft-repeated quadruple swellings downward which were visible as they scampered like mad across the floor."

While Ellen was creating a comfortable home, her husband was equally busy, vigorously arguing the political campaign of 1853 in his newspaper, the *Nevada Journal.* Aaron favored the policies of the Whigs, an early Republican-style party. An oppos-ing point of view was enthusiastically espoused by the newspaper *Young America*, which heralded the views of Democrats.

Ellen became worried in 1853 when the printed attacks on her husband became so heated he expected to be challenged to a duel. However, a friend, Judge David S. Belden, came to Aaron's defense before a challenge was issued. Editor R.A. Davridge of the rival newspaper *Young America* was threatening to shoot Aaron because of his strong political views. A crowd gathered. Judge Belden stepped in, drew his pistol, and announced he wanted to give a demonstration of his shooting skills. Using cards as targets Belden shot rapidly until the gun was empty, hitting a card with each shot.

He then announced he'd be happy to talk to anyone who didn't like Aaron Sargent, a man who had a family which he himself did not, and thus had nothing to lose if the discussion ended in an exchange of bullets. No one accepted.

In 1854, Aaron Sargent began the study of law. He studied alone, and in August of 1854, was admitted to the Bar of the District Court. He later served as district attorney and was the first resident of the county elected to the House of Representatives, serving three terms. He was also the first elected to the Senate and the only Nevada County resident to be appointed minister to Germany.

While her husband made his mark in the political world, Ellen Sargent was raising two children and building her own quiet legend. In addition to founding the first women's suffrage group in Nevada City in 1869, she served as president of similar organizations and presided at conventions called to gather women together to encourage them to continue the fight for the right to vote.

Fiery abolitionist and early feminist Susan B. Anthony visited the Sargent home in 1871. As a young Quaker, Susan Anthony had worked in the antislavery movement until passage of the Fourteenth Amendment in 1863 banned slavery in the United States. With that victory, she turned her attention to another case of unjust treatment in a land where all were said to be created equal: women's rights.

An editorial in the *New York Times* summed up the prevailing view of the "rights" of women at that time. "As for the spinster, we have often said that every woman has a natural and inalienable right to a good husband and a pretty baby. When, by 'proper agitation' (flirting) she has secured this right, she best honors herself and her sex by leaving public affairs behind her and by endeavoring to show how happy she can make the little world of which she has just become the brilliant center."

That editorial by Henry J. Raymond reflected the popular belief that employing her womanly wiles to catch a husband was proper for a female but employing her intelligence to decide civil matters like elections was not.

In a letter to a fellow suffragist in Palo Alto, Ellen reflected on the "great privileges and responsibilities of full American citizenship." She asked, "Does not that apply to women as well as men? Why cannot women see their low estate in the scale of humanity! And to think they could change it if they would. How their condition argues against their mentality and self-respect. Why do they not blush and arise in their might and inaugurate a true republic keeping with this enlightened age?"

When Aaron was elected to the US Senate, the Sargent family moved to Washington, D.C. Susan B. Anthony described accompanying the Sargent family on their journey to Washington in 1872. A huge snowfall on New Year's Day 1872 had brought the train to a standstill on the steepest upgrade of the Rockies. The trip from Laramie to Cheyenne, Wyoming, a distance of less than fifty miles, took five days. "Thankfully, the Sargents had brought along extra food and a spirit lamp for making tea," Susan wrote. They served tea and crackers to the nursing mothers on the train and comforted the passengers. However, Ellen herself was soon in need of comfort. "At Cheyenne, young Georgie Sargent got out to explore, slipped on the snow and broke his arm. Watching the painful bone-setting of her little son's arm, Ellen fainted."

Ellen and Susan B. Anthony visited and worked together many times in the nation's capital. In a letter to Mrs. Alice L. Park, a famous campaigner for women's rights, Ellen recalled her life in Washington. "I have many very pleasant memories of the place and the people I have met there. Mr. Sargent and myself, with our family, lived there twelve years. I learned a great deal while there; dined at the White House many times with distinguished people; visited at the Public Buildings; met Miss [Susan] Anthony, [Elizabeth Cady] Stanton, Isabella Beecher Hooker, all the other great lights of those times: love to think it over and appreciate the privilege more as time goes on."

Aaron died in 1887, after serving three terms in the House of Representatives and one in the Senate. He was best known for writing the bill that created the Transcontinental Railroad. After her husband's death, Ellen Sargent continued to work for the rights of women. She was an honorary president of the California Suffrage Association and a board member of the National American Women Suffrage Association.

In 1900, at the age of seventy-four, she went to court in a test case to protect the payment of property taxes. Her son, George, represented her in court, where she argued that since she was not allowed to vote, it was an instance of taxation without representation. That was, she argued, exactly the claim that started the Revolutionary War, which resulted in freedom from British rule. While the Declaration of Independence stated that all men are equal, suffragists argued that it was not meant to exclude women.

In the early twentieth century, Ellen was considered an influential pioneer suffragist, giving her time, energy, and money to advance the rights of women. She closely followed events in the state and the nation until her death on July 13, 1911, at the age of eighty-five. Ellen died at her home in San Francisco just two days after touring the city via automobile with her son-in-law. She lived an active life and always enjoyed visiting with friends and family, particularly her five grandchildren.

On July 25, 1911, more than two thousand suffragists assembled in Union Square to pay tribute to the memory of the gracious rebel. A program including band music, vocal solos, and speeches drew several hundred men to the bandstand, and the windows of the hotels and office buildings facing the square were filled with onlookers. The band played several patriotic songs, ending the interlude with "My Country 'Tis of Thee," in which the audience joined.

According to the July 26, 1911, edition of the *Oakland Tribune*, Congressman Thomas E. Hayden made the opening address praising Ellen Sargent's life and dedication, saying, "She was one of the wise women who saw years ago that women could not attain her highest development until she had the same large opportunities and the same large chance as her brothers have."

Ellen Sargent's funeral was held at her son George C. Sargent's residence at 251 Broadway in San Francisco. The question of where Ellen is buried remains a mystery. Historians at the California State Library in Sacramento speculate that she was laid to rest beside her husband at Laurel Hill Cemetery in San Francisco. In 1923, the cemetery was officially closed and a municipal ordinance was passed requiring the deceased be moved from the plots there. Many bodies were relocated to a cemetery in Coloma. Aaron Sargent's remains were moved to Nevada County, California, and a tombstone erected at Pioneer Cemetery. The location of Ellen's remains are yet unknown.

Baby Doe Tabor

d. 1935

This is the first instance where a lady, and such she is, has managed a mining property. The mine is doing very well and produces some rich ore.

—OCTOBER 1878 NEWS ARTICLE ON
HARVEY AND ELIZABETH DOE'S COLORADO GOLD MINE

A shabby-looking prospector emerged from the dark, weathered entrance of the Matchless Mine in Leadville, Colorado, and straightened his stooped shoulders. He dropped his pickax beside a rusty ore cart and rolled and lit a cigarette. His weary face was set in a scowl as he surveyed the mountains rising precipitously around the well-worked diggings. The smoke from the chimney of a nearby shack rose into the air and drifted toward him. As he watched the smoke swirl and evaporate into a vibrant blue sky, an elderly woman charged out the building into the cold. Seventy-five-year-old Baby Doe Tabor was dressed in layers of torn, threadbare garments that dragged along the ground as she walked. The woolen hat on her head sat just above her azure eyes, and she wore a ragged leather boot on one foot and a cluster of rags bound by a strip of material on the other. As she made her way toward the miner, a slight smile stretched across her hollowed cheeks. "What did you find?" she asked him hopefully. The man shook his head.

A flash of irritation erupted in her eyes but quickly dissipated as she scanned the colorful horizon.

Baby Doe's late husband was Horace Tabor, the Silver King. He made and lost a fortune in mining. At one time the country around her was swarming with workers who pulled millions out of the diggings where she lived. It had been more than thirty years since the mine had yielded anything but dust and rock. Baby Doe stayed on the property because of a deathbed promise she had made to Horace. "Never let the Matchless go if I die, Baby. It will make millions again when silver comes back."

She had implicit faith in her husband's judgment and in the Matchless, but she was alone in her belief. The only men who would agree to venture into the mine in 1929 were drifters or one-time hopeful prospectors. Baby Doe persuaded them to dig in exchange for shares in the potential find.

The disheveled miner took a look around, gathered up his few belongings, and tramped through the snow out of camp. Baby Doe's eyes followed the prospector until he disappeared into a grove of pine trees. "Hang on to the Matchless," she whispered to herself. "Horace told me it would make millions again."

The poverty and degradation that Baby Doe experienced in her last few years on earth were in direct contrast to the time she spent as the wife of a mining mogul. Born Elizabeth Bonduel McCourt in 1854 to a family of moderate means in Oshkosh, Wisconsin, she maneuvered her way around Colorado's high society until she met a man who would liberate her from her lackluster background. Her parents were Irish immigrants from County Armagh who had escaped the turmoil in their own country and initially settled in Utica, New York. They had fourteen children, many of whom died in infancy.

Elizabeth's angelic face, golden locks, and striking blue eyes set her apart from the other children. Her father, a tailor and the owner of a clothing store, doted on his daughter. Often he brought the child to work with him, and customers raved about the little girl's beauty. On more than one occasion, businessmen would ask if her father wasn't afraid "someone would steal her away." Baby Doe thrived on the attention of the male clientele and learned at a young age how to manipulate them into giving her whatever she asked for.

Elizabeth's stunning looks continued to improve as she got older. At fifteen she was five-foot-two, with long, blonde hair, a robust figure, and sun-kissed porcelain skin. Men of all ages hovered around her like frantic bees at a hive. She received several marriage proposals but refused the sincere suitors in favor of pursuing a career on the stage. She was also determined to wed a man of great wealth.

The bold teenager dismissed the admonitions of her brothers and sisters to behave sensibly, abandon the notion of acting, and settle down. Although there were a few respected actresses in the late 1870s, for the most part women thespians were considered to be a slight step above soiled doves. Elizabeth didn't care what "polite society" thought of her. She was driven by an independent spirit her father had nurtured and her dreams of fame and money.

In December 1876, Elizabeth participated in a skating contest hosted by the Congregational church. Boldly sporting a skirt that revealed her calves, she gracefully twirled through a routine, exciting the male onlookers and enraging female audience members. At the end of the competition, Elizabeth had captured a first-place ribbon and the heart of handsome socialite Harvey Doe.

Elizabeth was attracted to Harvey for a variety of reasons, not the least of which was the fact that he was heir to a mining dynasty. William Harvey Doe Sr. owned a substantial number of mining claims in Colorado.

Baby Doe Tabor, circa 1883 THE DENVER PUBLIC LIBRARY, WESTERN HISTORY COLLEC-
TION Z-231

Doe also owned a lumber business in Oshkosh and had returned with his son to check on his investment at the same time the skating event was being held. Harvey was quite smitten with Elizabeth, and her parents found the young man charming and personable. Mrs. Doe, however, objected to her son spending time with a girl she considered to be a "daring exhibitionist." Harvey disregarded his mother's complaints about Elizabeth's parents' financial standing and her view of the girl as a "social climber." He proclaimed his love for Elizabeth and proposed marriage.

Elizabeth's recollection of Harvey's proposal was that it was the first such invitation that had "moved her deeply." According to what she shared with a friend in the 1930s, Harvey was different from the other men in town who sought her affections. "He would come over to play the piano for all my family in the evening, seeming to love us all. He would join in the general fun without trying to monopolize me, like other men."

On June 27, 1877, Harvey and Elizabeth were married at her parents' home. Immediately after the ceremony the couple boarded a train bound for Denver, Colorado. Harvey Doe Sr. planned for his son to take over the mining property in nearby Central City.

Once the newlyweds had finished honeymooning they would embark on a life in the gold fields of Pike's Peak. Elizabeth's father-in-law made arrangements for her and her new husband to reside at a posh hotel called the Teller House. The inn was elegant and decorated with the finest European furniture and rugs.

Elizabeth was enthusiastic about her new home, and the luxurious living conditions were precisely what she had envisioned for herself. She was also enchanted with the activity at the Fourth of July Mine where Harvey worked. The sights and sounds of the miners descending into the diggings and reappearing with chunks of earth that might be gold stirred her desire for outrageous wealth.

At the time Elizabeth believed the opportunity to amass a fortune could only be realized through Harvey's efforts. Doe Sr.

wanted his son to earn his profits and reputation the same way he had, by working in every area of the mining development, from collecting ore to operating the stamp mill. Harvey, however, wasn't interested in manual labor and preferred anyone else to do the work. Elizabeth was far too ambitious to leave the future of her financial status to a lazy husband and quickly took command of their property and limited income.

After moving their belongings out of the expensive hotel where they had been living and into a small cottage, she organized a crew of Cornish miners to work at the Fourth of July Mine.

Some of the prominent town leaders with whom Elizabeth was acquainted advised her to have a shaft dug into the mine before winter fully set in. Joseph Thatcher, president of the First National Bank, and Bill Bush, owner of the Teller House, were two men whose opinion she respected the most. They urged her to do the digging herself if necessary.

Motivated by his wife's drive, Harvey finally bent to her will and joined in the work. The first shaft the pair sank proved to be unsuccessful as there was no high-grade ore in that section of the mine. Elizabeth was not going to give up. She convinced her husband and their employees to drive a second shaft. Dressed in one of Harvey's old shirts, a pair of dungarees, and a cap, Elizabeth toiled alongside the men.

In early October 1878, the editor of a mining newspaper in Central City was traveling through the busy area when he noticed the petite young woman lifting timbers and hauling tailings to a nearby pile. An article in the next edition of the paper included news about the woman prospector:

> *I next reached the Fourth of July lode, a mine which has not been worked for several years, but started up some months ago under the personal supervision of the owner, Mr. W. H. Doe and his wife. The young lady manages on half of the property while her liege lord manages the other.*

I found both of their separate shafts managing a number of workmen, Mr. Doe at his which is seventy feet, and his wife, who is full of ambition, in her new enterprise, at hers which is sunk sixty feet. This is the first instance where a lady, and such she is, has managed a mining property. The mine is doing very well and produces some rich ore.

For a brief moment it seemed that Elizabeth and Harvey were striving together for a common goal. The pair diligently worked their claim, leaving the mine only to collect supplies in town. Historians speculate that it was during one of those trips when Elizabeth acquired the name by which she would be more commonly known. Rough, outspoken miners congregated outside saloons and mercantiles, talking with one another and swapping stories about their prospecting adventures. As Elizabeth passed by the men on her way to purchase food and various odds and ends, one man called out, "There goes a beautiful baby." The handle suited her diminutive frame and delicate features, and from that time on she was referred to by most as "Baby Doe."

Despite their valiant efforts, the Fourth of July Mine never yielded the gold necessary to fund continued diggings. Harvey borrowed money to keep the operation going, but it was ultimately shut down. He went to work for another miner and abandoned his dream of striking it rich. Baby Doe held onto her aspiration of becoming a "woman of great means." She was determined to realize that dream with or without Harvey.

Baby voiced her disappointment to Harvey about his lack of business sense and drive, and he drank a lot as a way to cope with her criticism. They spent a great deal of time apart, he at the saloons and she at a fabric and clothing store called Sandelowsky-Pelton. Baby's father-in-law returned to the area to try to help the pair get beyond their financial difficulties. He sold the Fourth of July Mine and settled their outstanding debts, but it couldn't save

Baby and Harvey's relationship. By the summer of 1878, the two were leading virtually separate lives.

Baby spent a great deal of time with Jake Sandelowsky, the distinguished and handsome co-owner of the store she frequented. Her actions scandalized the town and infuriated Harvey. She defended Jake to her husband, making mention of the financial support the businessman had given her.

She wasn't shy about reminding Harvey that what she wanted most in life was financial independence. Desperate to save his marriage, Harvey worked extra shifts to provide his wife with a quality of life that would make her happy. Jake seized the time during his absence to shower Baby with attention. He was her frequent escort to a local theater and saloon called the Shoo-Fly. Jake tried to persuade her to leave Harvey and marry him, but he didn't possess the riches Baby hoped to make her own. She decided to remain married to Harvey until a truly better offer came along.

News that gold had been played out in Central City rapidly filtered through the Shoo-Fly clientele in November 1878. Silver veins had been located around the area, however, generating a surge of eager mine investors. Among the men with the capital to sink numerous shafts and extract the mineral was Horace Tabor. He had become rich with similar mines in Leadville and hoped to duplicate his success in Central City. Baby knew of Horace and had caught sight of the entrepreneur at the Shoo-Fly but had not been formally introduced. Before the possibility of a meeting was realized, Baby learned she was pregnant.

For several months Harvey was nowhere to be found and could not be told that he had a child on the way. There was some speculation that he had sneaked away to a nearby mining camp to avoid the humiliation of his wife's questionable behavior with another man. Harvey Doe Sr. located his son and brought him home to Baby.

On July 13, 1879, Baby gave birth to a boy. The child was stillborn, and both parents were crushed. Harvey was further devastated by the rumors circulating that the child might not have been his. Baby was discouraged by Harvey's inability to pay any of the medical bills or make arrangements for the infant's burial. Jake Sandelowsky came to Baby's rescue and took care of matters. The Does divorced in early 1880, and Baby left Central City for Leadville with Jake.

Jake and Baby lived at separate hotels. Although he had planned for their relationship to blossom, Baby had other ideas for her life. Everywhere she went in Leadville she heard stories about Horace Tabor. Tales of his wealth and how he achieved it, his benevolence to average citizens, his term as first mayor and postmaster of the city, his time as governor of Colorado, and his reputation as owner-operator of the Leadville Bank excited the industrious beauty from Wisconsin. She set her sights on meeting and befriending Horace. Jake would be a means to an end.

"He must be close to fifty," a friendly Leadville resident shared with Baby when she asked to know more about Horace. "They say he's worth $8 million and likes to play poker in the saloons around town after the theater lets out," the man continued. "He was one of the early prospectors out here, came in an ox-wagon across the plains in '59. An awful easygoing sort of fellow."

Baby listened intently to every detail of Tabor's life that the talkative local shared. She learned that the mine owner panned out his first millions in the gold stampede on Colorado's Gregory Gulch, that he grubstaked two miners who discovered a wealth of silver at the Little Pittsburgh Mine, and that he used the money from his investments to buy a claim called the Matchless Mine. She ignored the details about his longstanding marriage to a refined woman who possessed a considerable strength of character and focused instead on the name of the restaurant Horace frequented. It was not a coincidence that she ended up at the same establishment the "Silver King" visited during intermission at the Opera House.

"He was over six feet tall with large, regular features and a drooping mustache," Baby recounted years later to a young woman who spent time with her at her famous mine.

"Dark in coloring, at this time his hair had begun to recede a bit on his forehead and was turning gray at the temples. Always very well dressed, his personality seemed to fill any room he stepped into."

Horace noticed Baby almost from the moment he entered the eatery. They exchanged polite glances, and eventually one of his business associates invited Baby to join them at their table. Horace ordered champagne and regaled the captivated Baby with tales of his ventures west. "It was the merriest night of my life," Baby later confessed. By the end of the evening, she was convinced she was in love with Horace and he was equally as infatuated with her. He promised to support Baby monetarily, and, as his first order of business, he wrote out a check for $5,000 to help ease Jake Sandelowsky's soon-to-be broken heart. Funds were also provided for Baby to purchase herself a new wardrobe.

Within twenty-four hours of meeting the businessman and appointed governor, Baby had become Mr. Horace Tabor's mistress. They tried to keep their relationship a secret. Tabor would sneak away from various civic events to spend time with Baby at her hotel room, and when she appeared in public with him, she hid her face under large hats and long veils.

When Horace moved his mining offices from Leadville to Denver, Baby followed him. Friends and business associates aware of the scandalous romance tried to persuade him to end the affair for his family's sake and for the sake of his political future. Horace refused. The longer their relationship lasted, the bolder their behavior became. They traveled back and forth to Leadville together in private railcars and openly attended parties at various stops along the way.

Horace had a special box for Baby at the Opera House he had built. According to Baby Doe, at the opening of the Tabor Theatre on September 5, 1881, she and Horace eyed one another fondly during the performance. Horace's wife, Augusta, was eventually made aware of the affair, but refused to divorce her husband; she considered divorce a social and moral disgrace. After close to two years of pleading and negotiating with Augusta, Horace decided he and Baby Doe would exchange vows regardless of what Augusta did or didn't do.

On September 30, 1882, Baby Doe and Horace rendez-voused in St. Louis, Missouri, where they were secretly married by a justice of the peace. Although Baby was grateful that Horace had taken her to the altar, she was disappointed they weren't married in a church. "To me, a marriage was only binding when it had been sanctioned by the church and performed by a priest," Baby Doe recounted to a friend.

In January 1883, a few weeks prior to the senatorial election, in which Horace Tabor was a candidate, Augusta agreed to a legal divorce. The specifics of the settlement and circumstances leading up to Augusta's decision were front-page headlines. The highly publicized affair detracted from the real issues of the election and ultimately cost Horace a seat in the Senate. He was, however, asked to stand in for the winning candidate for a month until the newly elected official could take over his duties. It was with a heavy heart that Horace accepted the responsibility. Although he was disappointed in the vote, he found solace in the fact that he would soon be married in a church in Washington, D.C.

On March 1, 1883, Baby Doe was escorted down the aisle of St. Matthew's Catholic Church, wearing a $7,500 wedding dress and beaming at the attendees, including President Chester A. Arthur and the secretary of the interior, Henry Teller. The majority of the wives of the political figures who were guests at Horace and Baby's wedding refused to be a part of the ceremony in any

Horace Tabor THE DENVER PUBLIC LIBRARY, WESTERN HISTORY COLLECTION Z-22027

way. They spoke out against what they called an "unholy union" and considered it poor taste that the "shameless mistress" sent invitations at all.

Elated by the fact that they were now legally and finally married and optimistic that Horace's political career would be rejuvenated, the newlyweds returned to Denver. They moved into the Windsor Hotel and entertained celebrities and Civil War heroes in their suites. They traveled about the state, making stops at various mining camps in what the two secretly discussed as a precursor to a much larger tour coming their way once Horace became president of the United States. "First Lady of Colorado. Hell!" Horace told his wife. "You'll be first lady of the land."

In between making their elaborate plans for the future, the Tabors purchased the first of two grand, brick homes. The house featured fine furnishings, ornate verandas, driveways to the stables, and hundreds of live peacocks. An army of servants attended to the couple's every need. On July 13, 1884, Horace and Baby Doe brought their first child into the luxurious setting. The little girl's nursery was complete with an expensive layette and a sterling silver rattle. Employees at the Matchless Mine sent the child a gold-lined cup, saucer, and spoon. Horace sent small gold medallions to many of Denver's most prominent citizens to announce the birth of his daughter.

Regardless of the opulent living conditions and numerous attempts to obtain good standing in the social community, Baby and Horace were for the most part ostracized. Unable to find grace and acceptance within Denver's elite, Baby decided to focus solely on Horace and his mining claims. The Matchless Mine earned the Tabors more than $1 million annually and his other investments made more than $4 million. Horace used a substantial portion of the family's income to support the Republican Party in Colorado. He had hoped the hefty contribution would help him win a nomination for governor. Baby was frustrated with the treatment he received from the party, which in her opinion had no intentions of placing his name on the ticket. "They took his money and denied him any recognition," Baby lamented.

In his quest to become a man of unlimited power, Horace invested in mines in New Mexico, Arizona, Texas, and Latin America. He purchased forestland in Honduras, and he and Baby spent $2 million developing the property. Many of his risky ventures, including the Honduras project, lost millions.

Ten years after Horace and Baby were wed, the bottom fell out of the silver market, and overnight the Tabors lost all the wealth they had accumulated. "It seems incredible that it should have all happened so quickly," Baby later recalled, "but with one stroke of President Cleveland's pen, establishing the demonetization of silver, all of our mines, and particularly the Matchless, were worthless."

The Tabors were stripped of their possessions a little at a time over a six-month period. By December 1893, all that remained of their vast fortune was the Matchless Mine, and even that had to be shut down because the market would not support its yield. At sixty-three years old, Horace went to work as a regular laborer at a mine he had once owned. Baby tried to manage the minimal funds her husband brought in and cared for their two daughters. (In 1888 the Tabors had a son who lived only a few hours after his birth. Their second daughter was born in December 1889.)

When the Tabors were unable to pay their electric and water bill, workmen came to the house to shut off their utilities. Baby was livid and let her feelings be known.

"Just wait until Congress repeals the ridiculous law about the regulation of silver and the Matchless is running again," she told the workmen. "Then you'll be sorry you acted like this."

The Tabors moved into a small home on the west side of town. Denver's socialites gossiped about Horace and Baby's relationship, speculating on its longevity now that Horace was broke. Baby heard the rumors and insisted to all who would listen that she and Horace would stay together through the difficulties and rebuild their lives on the renewed success of the Matchless Mine.

According to Baby Doe, in late February 1898, she met with Colorado senator Ed Wolcott and pleaded with him to help her and her family. Wolcott knew Baby from her days in Central City and Leadville, and he and Horace had squared off politically on several occasions. It was because of Senator Wolcott's efforts that Horace was appointed as Denver's postmaster. The job paid $3,500 a year and helped restore a modicum of dignity to Horace's life. Baby was overjoyed. She believed it was an indication that their luck had changed and that their old life would soon be restored, but harder times were yet to come.

On April 3, 1899, Horace died from an acute appendicitis attack. Baby was at his side when he passed away. With his last breath he encouraged his wife to hold onto the Matchless Mine. Cards and letters of condolence poured in from national and state

Baby Doe Tabor in Denver, circa early 1920s THE DENVER PUBLIC LIBRARY, WEST-
ERN HISTORY COLLECTION Z-232

political leaders. Flags across Colorado were ordered to be flown at
half-mast. Out of respect for the years Horace had spent as a political servant in the state of Colorado, thousands of mourners lined
Denver's streets to see Horace's funeral procession. After a graveside service, Horace was laid to rest at the Calvary Cemetery. He
was later moved to the Mount Olive Cemetery when the Calvary
Cemetery was dissolved.

With Horace gone, the grief-stricken Baby decided to focus
her efforts on finding investors to back the reopening of the
Matchless Mine. Having been unworked for many years, the mine
was filled with water and initial funds were needed to pump the
liquid out, stabilize the tunnels, and purchase new machinery. After
an exhaustive search, Baby located a businessman who fronted
her the capital to begin operations. Baby moved her fifteen- and

nine-year-old daughters, Elizabeth Lillie and Rose, to Leadville where the Matchless Mine was located, and she went to work hiring help to support the dig. She encouraged her children to learn all the aspects of running the mine, from swinging a pick to hauling ore to the surface, but her eldest daughter refused to ever have any part of it.

When the Matchless Mine failed to produce any significant gold, the investor withdrew his support, forcing Baby to search for other backers. This scenario was repeated time and time again. She refused to give up or sell the property outright, and for three decades she steadfastly maintained that riches were buried deep within the walls of the mine. Her children grew up and moved on, but Baby remained in Colorado in a dilapidated cabin located at the site. "I shall never let the Matchless go," she told a banker she was asking to back the mine operations. "Not while there is a breath in my body to find a way to fight for it."

When the money ran out, Baby worked the mine alone. Occasionally she sold off a few of Horace's valuables (such as watch fobs, and cufflinks) to buy food and clothing. Both of her daughters, tired of their mother's obsession with the Matchless, distanced themselves from her. Elizabeth Lillie married and moved to Wisconsin; Rose ("Silver Dollar," as her mother called her) drifted to Chicago where she was murdered at the age of thirty-five. With the exception of a neighbor and benevolent mine engineer and his daughter, Baby Doe lived the life of a recluse, visited by no one. The journal she kept in her later days describes how lonely she was and how much she missed Horace and her children. An entry she made on April 19, 1925, reads "Holy Thursday. Dreamed of being with Tabor, Lillie, and Silver and seeing rich ore in No. 6 shaft."

In 1932, a movie about the life and career of Horace Tabor, entitled *Silver Dollar*, premiered in Denver. It generated new interest in the Tabor legacy and in his affair with Baby Doe. Press agents and historians sought out Baby to interview her and per-

Horace and Elizabeth Tabor's tombstone COURTESY DEVIN SCHROEDER

suade her to tell her story in exchange for a fee, but she refused. She maintained that any money worth making, the Matchless Mine would ultimately supply.

On February 20, 1935, Baby Doe Tabor, the woman once known throughout the West as the "Silver Queen," died. A severe blizzard blanketed Leadville with snow and ice, and Baby, who was suffering from pneumonia, was unable to keep a fire going in her cabin. Her neighbors became concerned about her when they didn't see any smoke emanating from the chimney. Her frozen body was found lying on the floor of her rundown cabin, her arms outstretched at her side.

Funeral services for Baby Doe were held at a church in Leadville, and her remains were then taken to Denver to be buried next to Horace. The headline across the front of the *Rocky Mountain* newspaper read, "Baby Doe Dies at Her Post Guarding Matchless Mine." The article that followed reported on the squalid conditions of her home and noted that only a "small cache of food and a few sticks of firewood" were found on the premises.

Among the personal belongings she left behind were seventeen trunks filled with a variety of memorabilia, including scrapbooks, old newspapers, and a silver Tiffany tea set. Sue Bonnie, the daughter of the mine engineer who called on Baby from 1927 until her death, used Baby Doe's scrapbook and journal entries, along with their documented conversations, to write a series of articles. From January to May of 1938, the articles about Baby Doe and her recollections of life as a miner and her marriage to Horace Tabor were published in *True Story* magazine.

Baby Doe Tabor was eighty-one years old when she passed away. The onetime heiress to a vast silver empire had remained faithful to her husband's parting advice for thirty-six years. Baby Doe was buried next to her husband at Mount Olivet Cemetery in Jefferson County, Colorado.

William Tilghman

d. 1924

He died for the state he helped create. He set an example
of modesty and courage that few could match, yet he made
us all better men for trying.

— GOVERNOR MARTIN E. TRAPP SPEAKING AT
THE FUNERAL OF BILL TILGHMAN

Legendary lawman and sportswriter Bat Masterson once referred to his well-known colleague Bill Tilghman as "the finest among us all." Marshall Tilghman and Sheriff Bat Masterson were two members of the "most intrepid posse" of the Old West, a group of policemen who, in 1878, tracked down the killer of a popular songstress named Dora Hand.

William Matthew Tilghman Jr.'s drive to legitimately right a wrong began at an early age. He was born on the Fourth of July 1854 in Fort Dodge, Iowa. His father was a soldier turned farmer, and his mother was a homemaker. Bill spent his early childhood in the heart of the Sioux Indian territory in Minnesota. Grazed by an arrow when he was a baby, he was raised to respect Native Americans and protect his family from tribes that felt they had been unfairly treated by the government.

Bill was one of six children. His mother insisted he had been "born to a life of danger."

In 1859 his family moved to a homestead near Atchison, Kansas. While Bill's father and oldest brother were fighting in the Civil War, he worked the farm and hunted game. One of the most significant events in his early life occurred when he was twelve years old while returning home from a blackberry hunt. His hero, Bill Hickok, rode up beside him and asked if he had seen a man ride through with a team of mules and a wagon.

The wagon and mules had been stolen in Abilene, and the marshal had pursued the culprit across four hundred miles. Bill told Hickok that the thief had passed him on the road that led to Atkinson. The marshal caught the criminal before he left the area and escorted him back to the scene of the crime. Bill was so taken by Hickok's passion for upholding the law that he decided to follow in his footsteps and become a scout and lawman.

From 1871 to 1888, Bill hunted buffalo, rounded up livestock, scouted for the military, and operated a tavern in Dodge City, Kansas. In 1889, Bill settled in Oklahoma and was at once appointed deputy US marshal, thus taking to a calling that made him famous as a hustler of outlaws of the most desperate kind. During his term in office, he amassed a fortune in rewards paid by the government for the capture of such noted desperados, train robbers, bank robbers, and murderers as Bill Doolin, Tulsa Jack, Bitter Creek, and Bill Dalton.

In his many years of continuous service as US marshal, Bill was the associate of such noted scouts as Luke Short, Pat Garrett, Wild Bill Hickok, Neal Brown, and Charley Bassett. Bat Masterson was also one of the famous marshals of Dodge City in the early days and knew Bill Tilghman well. The two were lifelong friends. Masterson once said of Tilghman, "After a career of sixteen years on the firing lines of America's last frontier and after being shot at five hundred times by the most desperate outlaws in the land,

William Tilghman RESEARCH DIVISION OF THE OKLAHOMA HISTORICAL SOCIETY

whose unerring aim with a six-shooter or Winchester seldom failed to bring down their victims, this man, Bill Tilghman, came through it all unscathed, and is perhaps the only frontiersman who has been constantly on the job for more than a generation and lives to tell the tale."

Bill Tilghman was twice elected sheriff of Lincoln County, Oklahoma, after which he was elected to the state senate, resigning that office to accept the job of chief of police of Oklahoma City. He would resign that position in 1914 to campaign for US marshal in Oklahoma. Bill received the appointment and rendered valuable service not only during that term but also at various other times he had the post.

In 1924 Bill was persuaded to take on the job of cleaning up a lawless oil boomtown called Cromwell in Oklahoma. He was seventy-one years old when he was shot in an ambush on Saturday, November 1, 1924, by a corrupt Prohibition enforcement officer. Wiley Lynn, the man who shot the aged officer, fled the scene of the crime but gave himself up to authorities in Holdenville, Oklahoma. Lynn admitted to officers at Holdenville that he shot Bill, but would make no further statement. He was placed in the Hughes County jail to await formal action by the authorities.

Cromwell had long been known as a "wide open" town. Dance halls and gambling joints had been running freely, and booze was easy to obtain. Vice conditions were regarded as so bad that federal authorities had been dispatched to the area. Lynn was one of a handful of agents sent to the territory.

Conditions in Cromwell did not get any better with the presence of the federal authorities. When the situation escalated, a step toward more law enforcement was made, and Bill was called in to serve in the role in which he had gained fame. Now he no longer was the Bill of the old days when his daring speed on the trigger made him respected and feared by all law breakers. Conditions improved somewhat, however, and there were indications that a complete cleanup there might be made.

The fatal shooting occurred when Bill attempted to place under arrest members of a motorcar party who were disturbing the peace on the main street of town. One of the men fired a pistol shot into the air, and a few minutes later spectators heard angry words and another shot. Bill fell and was dead before anyone reached him.

After shooting Marshal Tilghman, the slayer fled in the car, occupied by another man and two women, and drove rapidly out of town. Wiley Lynn was arrested and tried for killing Bill, but was found not guilty of murder. The jury believed he had acted in self-defense.

Eight years after killing Marshal Tilghman, Wiley Lynn died in a gun battle with Oklahoma State Bureau of Investigation agent Crockett Long in Mandill, Oklahoma. On July 17, 1932, an inebriated Lynn confronted Agent Crockett with his pistol drawn. The agent quickly drew his weapon, and the two fired at one another at the same time. Both Agent Crockett and Wiley Lynn died as a result of gunshot wounds.

Graveside services for lawman Bill Tilghman were held at Oak Park Cemetery in Lincoln County, Oklahoma.

William Alexander Anderson Wallace

d. 1899

Here Lies He Who Spent His Manhood Defending the Homes of Texas. Brave, Honest, and Faithful.

— Grave marker inscription for William Wallace

Texas Ranger, hunter, and adventurer William Alexander Anderson Wallace, better known as Big Foot Wallace, died on January 7, 1899, near Devine, Texas, but the legendary Texas Ranger's body was taken to the state cemetery in Austin to be buried. The man many referred to as the Daniel Boone of Texas was so well respected by the people of the state they wanted him to be laid to rest in a place of honor.

Born in Virginia on April 13, 1817, the six-foot-two Wallace came to Texas in 1836, soon after the battle of San Jacinto, which freed Texas from Mexican rule. His brother and other relatives from Georgia were massacred by the Mexican army at Goliad, Texas. He became a captain of the Texas Rangers and was also a soldier in the US–Mexican War of 1846.

Wallace was a romantic character coming to Texas in frontier days; he sought adventure and courted danger of the hair-raising type. Whether fighting wild animals, Indians, Mexicans, or white bandits, he was always cool and deadly under fire.

In 1842, Wallace joined the ill-fated Mier Expedition, the last of the raiding expeditions from Texas into Mexico during the days of the Republic. The expedition was an attempt to overtake Mexican settlements. Wallace was captured by Mexican soldiers and thrown into a cell with several other prisoners from the mission. The captives were treated cruelly, hitched as horses to carts and made to haul gravel for streets in the town where they were held. Big Foot Wallace was a docile "horse" for one trip, and then he went wild, snorted, kicked, pitched, turned his cart over into a ditch and broke it into pieces. The guards took the recalcitrant horse-man out of the harness.

A lottery scheme in which the stakes were life and death by drawing white and black beans is, perhaps, the best known episode in the life of Big Foot Wallace. Wallace and the other prisoners were escorted by their Mexican captors from Ciudad Mier to Mexico City. Before they reached Mexico City, however, some of the Texans, including Wallace, managed to escape. The escapees ended up lost in the mountains west of Monterey, and many died of thirst. Those who survived were recaptured.

Santa Anna, the Mexican general, ordered every tenth man of the recaptured prisoners shot as a punishment for escaping. A pot of seventeen black and one-hundred-fifty-two white beans was given to the uncooperative prisoners. There was a black bean for every tenth man. Drawing a white bean meant life, while drawing a black bean meant death to the prisoners. A young man from Mississippi drew a fatal black bean. He lost his nerve and wept bitterly. Through his tears he cried out how broken-hearted he was over the fact that he would never see his mother again. Wallace handed the youth a white bean and went back to the pot and drew another white bean.

Shortly after the seventeen prisoners were killed, the Mexican soldiers chained the hands of survivors together and forced them

William Alexander Anderson Wallace

at gunpoint to continue the trip to Mexico City. By the time the prisoners reached San Luis Potosí, both of Wallace's arms were swollen from the tightness of his chains. The wife of a Mexican government official saw the condition Wallace was in and ordered that his chains be removed.

In Mexico City the Texans were greeted by a jeering crowd. Wallace stood up to the people and bit one of the disapproving citizens in the neck. The mob scattered and never troubled the Texan again. Wallace and the other prisoners were interned at the Castle of Perote, the strongest prison in Mexico. In late 1844, after more than twenty-two months in prison, Wallace and the rest of the Texan captives were released.

At Veracruz, Wallace boarded a condemned ship headed for New Orleans and immediately contracted yellow fever. Once his health was restored, he joined a cattle drive to San Antonio. He established a small farm on the Medina River in south central Texas in 1845. In addition to raising modest crops of vegetables, Wallace was also an avid hunter, and his primary game was panther. He served as a frontier scout and tracker, and led manhunts to help settlers locate children taken by Indians. On September 28, 1845, Wallace enlisted as a Texas Ranger and served until June 26, 1846; he then fought in the Mexican War, and rejoined the Rangers again in July 1846.

After a successful period as a Ranger, protecting settlers from Indians, outlaws, and Mexicans, Wallace returned to his home near the Medina River. Off and on he fought Indians with his friend and fellow Ranger, Edward Dixon Westfall. Wallace also took time away from farming and hunting to drive a mail stage. Once a month, from 1850 to 1858, he drove the mail from San Antonio to El Paso.

In 1859, Captain Wallace went back to Virginia to visit relatives. When he returned he discovered that a band of Comanche Indians had swept through the Sabinal and Hondo country, killing and rustling. Big Foot was made leader of a posse to track them. Unfortunately, his men were green and stubborn. In the famous battle on Seco Creek that followed, they jumped into ambushes that Big Foot warned them about and spoiled the ambushes he laid for the Indians. After two days of hard fighting, Wallace was disgusted. The Indians had been run off, but not wiped out, and to Wallace that was no victory.

In 1861, Texas seceded from the Union by popular vote. When the Civil War began, Wallace didn't participate, because he didn't see a reason to join. Instead, he stayed in Texas and helped families whose loved ones did participate in the War between the States. Wallace's services to the state were rewarded by the grant of 120 acres of public land, and a town was named after him.

In 1874, another force of Texas Rangers was organized. Wallace was sixty years old but still capable of doing the job.

During his last years he lived with friends and made one last trip—this one to the reunion of old Rangers at the state fair in Dallas. He was eighty-two years old. Shortly after the reunion Wallace passed away. He was interred at the Texas State Cemetery.

Winema

d. 1920

I am a Modoc myself. I am here to talk peace. Shoot me if you dare, but I will never betray you.

—WINEMA'S CHALLENGE TO FELLOW MODOC TRIBE MEMBERS

Mrs. Frank "Tobey" Riddle, better known as Winema, was a mediator between the Modoc people, other Indian tribes in the area of Klamath Lake, Oregon, and the US Army in early 1878. With her skills she was able to negotiate treaties that kept the land of her ancestors in peace. Whenever that peace was threatened, her job was to set things straight. In February 1873, she rode into hostile Modoc territory to persuade the chief to surrender to the US cavalry.

Chief Keintpoos, or Captain Jack (a name given to him by the settlers because of his fondness for brass buttons and military medals on his coat), was Winema's cousin. In 1863 the US government forced his people from their land onto a reservation in Oregon. Conditions on the reservation were intolerable for the Modoc people. They were forced to share the land with the Klamath Indians of the region. The Modoc and the Klamath did not get along. The Modoc struggled to live in this hostile environment for three years. Modoc leaders appealed to the US government to separate the tribes, but officials refused to correct the problem. In 1869, Captain Jack defied the laws of the white man and led his tribe off the reservation and back to the area where their forefathers had first lived.

The cavalry and frustrated members of the Indian Peace Council wanted to use force to bring Captain Jack and his followers back to the reservation. Winema persuaded them instead to give her a chance to talk with the chief.

When Winema reached the Modoc camp, Captain Jack's men gathered around her. A dozen pistols were drawn upon her as she dismounted. She eyed the angry tribesmen as they slowly approached her. Then walking backward until she stood upon a rock above the mobs, she clasped her right hand upon her own pistol, and with the other on her heart she shouted aloud, "I am a Modoc myself. I am here to talk peace. Shoot me if you dare, but I will never betray you." Her bravery in the face of such difficulty won the admiration of her people, and instantly a dozen pistols were drawn in her defense.

Winema was born near the Link River in Oregon. Her mother died in childbirth. She was raised by her father, older sister, and brother. She was regarded by her people as an extraordinary young woman. The elders of the tribe told her stories of her heritage; her father took her on grizzly bear hunts and taught her Modoc traditions. While she was still a girl, she encountered a white settler—an experience that fired her heart to learn all she could about the white man's history and how it differed from her own.

This particular white man had been on his way to Oregon when he got separated from his wagon train and became lost. When Winema and her father happened on the man, he was alone and starving. They helped him to their village and nursed him back to health. While recuperating, he shared stories with Winema

Winema NATIONAL ANTHROPOLOGICAL ARCHIVES, SMITHSONIAN INSTITUTION [03051-A]

about the great cities and towns in the East and of his wonderful civilization and their achievements. Winema was fascinated.

Occasionally, members of the Modoc tribe would visit the miners in and around Yreka, California. It was on one of those visits that Winema first met the man who would become her husband, Frank Riddle. Frank was a prospector, bent on finding the mother lode. He had left his betrothed in Kentucky with the promise that he would return with his weight in gold and marry her on the spot. He never imagined a Native woman would steal his heart. The two were wed a few short weeks after meeting.

Frank and Winema made their home on a ranch not far from Yreka, but there was no peace for the two or the land. Several tribes in the southern portion of Oregon were at war. Many bloody battles were being fought near the Riddles' homestead and at times in the streets of town. Driven by the unrest in the area and saddened by the Natives' inability to get along, Winema took it upon herself to act as mediator among the tribes and, at times, between her own race and the white man. She organized a treaty council and enlisted members of the fighting bands to participate in peace talks. An agreement was reached among all parties, and for a time bloodshed was avoided. Winema was known by all in the territory as "the one who could make peace, and who always calmed the threatening tempest arising from contact of races."

Less than a year after a peace treaty was agreed upon, the US government defied the terms by refusing to recognize Captain Jack as chief of the Modoc people. The government had also violated the treaty by forcing members of the Klamath tribe to share reservation land with the Modoc. Believing the agreement between the Modoc and the United States broken, Captain Jack felt justified in leaving the reservation.

A peace commission made up of three government officials was dispatched to Yreka. It comprised General Edward Canby, Methodist preacher Eleazar Thomas, and a onetime superintendent of the Modoc reservation Albert Meacham. Meacham knew that Winema and Captain Jack were related and asked her for help in persuading the chief to return to the reservation. Winema agreed, but Captain Jack would not relent. Finally, in 1873, four years after the Modoc chief led his people off their designated land and after seeing his cousin's courage as she faced his warriors on the rock, he gave in to Winema's request.

The first meeting between Captain Jack and the government officials took place in early spring 1873. Winema took her place beside her cousin, across from Canby, Thomas, and Meacham. She rendered their English into Modoc, and, after several tense moments, the question on the commission's mind was asked.

Winema studied the chief's face, waiting for him to respond. "Will I go back to the reservation?" Captain Jack repeated dully. "All right," he continued, "provided my people be given Modoc Point on the Klamath reservation for our home." Meacham and the others agreed. They celebrated the end of the conflict by cheering and patting one another on the back. Captain Jack took offense at the demonstration and jumped to his feet. His braves drew their pistols on the unsuspecting commission. Winema reacted quickly, placing herself between the government officials and the Indians. She quickly defused the situation. The meeting ended with the Modoc chief and all his people returning to the reservation.

Within a few short weeks, however, trouble on the reservation escalated again. The lives of Captain Jack and his people were constantly being threatened by members of the Klamath tribe, it seemed, and the US government was not providing the Modoc with protection. Captain Jack and followers left the reservation for a second time; no amount of talking from members of the peace commission would entice them to change their minds.

Major Jackson of the US Cavalry was organizing his troops for an attack against Captain Jack and his braves when Winema made a final appeal for a nonviolent resolution. "If you take these

Modoc by force," she told the major, "no peace could ever be made." Jackson waited until two of his divisions had surrounded Captain Jack's camp before it was agreed that another set of peace talks was in order. Winema was dispatched to the Modoc camp to make the arrangements for the meeting.

Captain Jack did not welcome his cousin with the same warmth as he had in the past. He scarcely made a move to protect her when the braves greeted her with loaded weapons. He was furious about the government's broken promises and, at first, would not listen to Winema's request for another meeting with the government officials. After several hours of taunting her with the breaches of the contract for peace negotiations, he agreed to meet with the commission the following day. Something in his countenance made Winema suspicious of his motives. She left the camp feeling uneasy about what lay ahead.

On April 11, 1873, General Canby, the Reverend Eleazar Thomas, and Albert Meacham made their way to the site where they were to meet with Captain Jack. Winema rode with them. The peace commission had agreed to come to the meeting unarmed, a notion with which she strongly disagreed. She tried to convince Canby that they should be cautious. "Captain Jack and his braves do not trust any longer," she told the general. "There could be trouble." General Canby suggested that Winema was wrong and only frightened by her experience with Captain Jack the day before.

The tension inside the tent where the talks were to be held was thick. The peace commission sat on one side, Captain Jack and his men on the other. Winema placed herself between them all. Captain Jack was the first to speak. "Will you remove the soldiers from our land and give my people a home in the country?" he asked. "If the soldiers should be removed, the phantom of death would pass as a dream," he continued. "If they should not be withdrawn, the phantom must soon become a terrible reality."

The three members of the peace commission fearfully looked on. With dignity befitting a soldier of his standing, General Canby pronounced firmly, "I cannot withdraw the soldiers."

Winema watched the anger intensify in Captain Jack's eyes as she interpreted the general's response. In one fast instant Captain Jack drew a pistol and shot General Canby in the face. One of the Modoc braves fired a shot at Thomas, hitting him in the hand. He jumped to his feet and started out of the tent. Another Indian shot him in the back of the head. By the time the violence turned to Albert Meacham, Winema had thrown herself in front of him. With her arms outstretched, she pleaded for his life. A brave pushed her out of the way and put a bullet through Meacham's left eye, blinding him. Winema lay down on top of Meacham, shouting, "Don't shoot anymore!"

Captain Jack and his braves rushed out the tent, leapt onto their horses, and rode off. Winema wiped the blood from Meacham's face and straightened his limbs. She believed he was dead. She looked around at the bodies of Thomas and Canby. They had been scalped and stripped of their clothing.

Winema rushed out the tent. Looking south, she saw her cousin and his comrades on horseback racing away from the scene. Winema made her way to the commanding officer of the cavalry and explained what happened. The bodies of General Canby and the Reverend Thomas were buried outside the cavalry post. Albert Meacham was removed to the camp hospital. His wounds were pronounced dangerous but not mortal.

The Modoc War lasted several weeks. The cavalry launched full-scale attacks against the Modoc braves holed up in the rocks around the army camp. On May 22, 1873, the US Cavalry finally broke the Modoc, and the braves surrendered, offering to lead the soldiers to Captain Jack. The Indian chief and five other warriors were arrested for the murder of General Canby and the Reverend Eleazar Thomas. They were tried, found guilty, and sentenced to death.

Winema returned to the Modoc reservation in Oregon to live out the rest of her life. In 1890 she was granted a pension by the federal government as a reward for her years of work to bring about peace. She donated the majority of the money to her people. She died in 1920 at the age of eighty-four and was buried in Modoc Cemetery. A national forest in south-central Oregon is named for the tenacious woman chief.

Victoria Claflin Woodhull

d. 1927

As I look back over childhood to maturity, I realize that
there was some subtle power of transmutation at work, for
somehow, from the very first moment, I seemed to know
all the future without being able to give any expression in
words.

—Reminiscence of Victoria Claflin in *Notorious Victoria*

When Victoria Claflin Woodhull died on June 9, 1927, news of her passing was announced on two continents. The press referred to the controversial writer, stockbroker, and politician as a "most immoral woman." Not only was Victoria the first woman to be officially nominated for president of the United States, but she was also one of the first individuals to have been jailed on federal obscenity charges. Both events occurred in 1872.

Before her involvement with the women's rights movement, Victoria and her sister, Tennessee, were the owners and publishers of a newspaper called the *Woodhull and Claflin Weekly.* They printed scandalous articles promoting the idea of "free love." In a letter Victoria sent to the *New York Times* in 1871, she claimed that free love was the "only cure for immorality, the deep damnation by which men corrupt and disfigure God's most holy institution of sexual relations." She continued, "It is not marriage but sexual intercourse, then, that is God's most holy institution." Victoria and Tennessee's progressive views on sex and the brazen printing of those ideals appalled citizens not only in the United States but also in other countries like Germany and Russia. They "threaten to destroy the morals nations so desperately needed to cling to," was the opinion voiced in the *New York Times* on November 23, 1871.

Victoria and Tennessee were not strangers to confrontation with the law. Their father, Reuben Buckman "Buck" Claflin, was a scoundrel who excelled at breaking the rules of conventional society and spent time behind bars for his actions. Buck and his wife, Roxanna Hummel, lived in a rundown house in Homer, Ohio. The couple had ten children. Born on September 23, 1838, Victoria was the Claflins' sixth child. Although Victoria's father claimed to be a lawyer with his own profitable practice, he was actually a skilled thief with no law degree at all. He owned and operated a gristmill and also worked as a postmaster. Buck supplemented his income by stealing from merchants and business owners, and he was a counterfeiter and a suspected arsonist.

Victoria's mother was a religious fanatic who dismissed Buck's illegal activities in favor of chastising her neighbors for what she claimed was hedonism. Her public prayers were loud, judgmental, and dramatic. She preached to her children and insisted they memorize long passages of the Old Testament. By the time Victoria was eight, she was able to recite the Bible from cover to cover. Reflecting on her life, Victoria wrote in *Autobiography of Victoria Claflin* that her mother's spiritual zeal so influenced her childhood that young Victoria believed she could see into the future and predict what was to come of those who sought her out to preach.

Tennessee was reported to be the true clairvoyant of the family. Born in 1845, she was the last child born to Roxanna

Victoria Woodhull MARY MCCARTHY PAPERS, ARCHIVES & SPECIAL COLLECTIONS LIBRARY, VASSAR COLLEGE (REF#3.884 WOODHULL, V.)

and Buck. Roxanna claimed Tennessee had the power to perceive things not present to the senses. She would slip into trances and speak with spirits, answering voices no one else could hear.

Victoria and Tennessee had very little formal education. Although Victoria attended school for only four years, she was bright, precocious, and well read. She was uninhibited and at the age of eleven delivered sermons from a busy location in Homer, Ohio.

In 1849, the Claflins left Homer and moved to Mount Gilead, Ohio. Victoria's father had abandoned gristmill work and decided to venture into the field of psychic phenomena with his daughters in tow. He introduced Victoria and Tennessee to the public and announced the girls' talent for "second sight" or "extrasensory perception, the ability to receive information in the form of a vision by channeling spirits." Buck rented a theater and charged patrons seventy-five cents to watch the four-year-old and eleven-year-old communicate with deceased Claflin family members and predict the future. One such specific prediction was that one day a woman would be president of the United States.

Victoria and Tennessee's shows, in which they would conduct séances and interpret dreams for audience members, attracted a large following, and in a short time the two young girls became the sole source of income for their family.

At the age of fifteen, Victoria married a twenty-eight-year-old doctor named Canning Woodhull. The doctor had moved to Mount Gilead from Rochester, New York, to set up a practice. The pair met when Victoria's parents asked Canning to treat Victoria when she was suffering from rheumatism and a fever. Five months after nursing his patient back to health, the two were married. They exchanged vows on November 20, 1853. The Woodhulls' marriage was a troubled one—the doctor was an alcoholic and had numerous affairs.

The Woodhulls moved to San Francisco, California, in 1855, in hopes that the change of scenery would improve their marital condition. It did not. Victoria's husband refused to find steady employment. With her baby in tow, Victoria found odd jobs, including selling cigars and working as a seamstress. Three years after the Woodhulls moved to San Francisco, Victoria claimed to have received a vision of her sister Tennessee calling for her to return home. She wasted no time packing her family's things, boarding a steamship, and traveling back to Ohio.

Buck Claflin had made arrangements for his daughters to perform their supernatural gifts at a theater in Columbus, Ohio. He encouraged the women to listen closely to individual audience members' requests and con them into giving them large sums of money to heal serious diseases or minor ailments or to predict the outcome of a specific event. Victoria let her father know that their natural gifts would be enough to sustain the family financially, but did not refuse to defraud many ticket holders. In 1859, the sister act of Woodhull and Claflin earned more than $100,000.

Victoria and Tennessee toured most of the Midwest's big cities and their traveling medicine show attracted the attention of not only the frail and desperate but also law enforcement. Authorities were concerned that the sisters were charlatans and would have to be stopped. "The sisters were superbly equipped for a career in the shadowy realm that lies between complete [integrity] and outright crime," a report in the March 9, 1864, edition of the *Oakland Tribune* noted. "They peddled a magic elixir . . . with Tennessee's picture on the bottle. They were making a nice living."

The Woodhulls' marriage continued to be mired in infidelity and mistrust. Victoria prayed for another child in the hope that a baby free from any mental or physical problems might make things better between her and her husband. The Woodhulls' son was afflicted with mental retardation. She claimed it happened from a head injury he received as a child when her husband dropped the baby. He claimed that she was an alcoholic and caused the child's retardation by drinking while pregnant. In the spring of

1861, Zula Maude was born. Victoria and Canning doted on their daughter, but the baby could not repair the damage already done. Victoria had spent six years blaming and berating her husband for their son's condition. Historian Herb Michelson noted in an article in the March 9, 1964, edition of the *Oakland Tribune* that "Victoria brought Woodhull untold misery for the role she believed he played in their child's handicap, and he became a human derelict as a result." The Woodhulls separated in 1864.

The demise of Victoria's marriage did not distract her from her work. She continued to mesmerize audiences with her so-called powers of mystical observation. While her divorce was being finalized, Victoria appeared on stage without Tennessee. Buck decided the family income could be doubled if the act was separated. He booked the women in different theaters, and, as predicted, their earnings were twice as large. A run-in with the law in June 1864 threatened to bring an end to the performances by Woodhull and Claflin and bankrupt the family. At a show in Pittsburgh, Pennsylvania, Tennessee laid hands on an audience member suffering from cancer and told the woman she had healed her. The ailing woman died a few weeks after the program, however, and authorities planned to charge Tennessee with manslaughter. Buck and the rest of the family fled the scene before an arrest could be made. Victoria and Tennessee then traveled to Cincinnati, Ohio. While there Victoria persuaded her sister to let her manage their careers instead of their father. Tennessee agreed.

The attractive sister act took to the stage again, showing off their clairvoyant talent and promoting a tonic that promised to cure any ailment and lift the spirits. Law enforcement officers responded to complaints that the tonic the women were selling was more alcohol than medicine. Accusations were also made that Victoria and Tennessee were running a brothel and were adulteresses and blackmailers—claims Victoria vehemently denied. According to the September 30, 1871, edition of the *Anglo-American Times,*

Victoria reported that the allegations were made by "skeptical women whose husbands frequented Woodhull and Claflin performances." Hoping to shake the rumors that plagued them in Cincinnati, Victoria and her sister made their way to Chicago. Within a month of arriving in Illinois, Victoria was in trouble with the law again, this time for fraudulent fortune-telling.

Victoria fled to Tennessee with her sister, and, in late 1864, the pair joined a medicine show their father had organized that was touring the area. The freight wagon carrying Victoria and her children, parents, and siblings stopped at small towns that had been ravaged by the Civil War. Woodhull and Claflin preyed on families dealing with the devastating loss of loved ones. Promising to rid communities of diseases such as cancer, cholera, and diphtheria, Victoria and Tennessee laid their hands on the sick and frail, recited a mysterious incantation, and sent them on their way. The sisters made the ailing believe their illnesses would be gone in twenty-four hours.

In April 1865, the medicine show rolled into St. Louis, Missouri. Tired of living and working out of a wagon, Victoria rented a hotel suite for herself and her two children. Many people seeking to speak with their sons, brothers, and husbands who had been killed in the Civil War called on Victoria for help. Colonel James H. Blood, commander of the 6th Army and St. Louis's newly elected city auditor, was one of many people who visited Victoria at her suite. He needed Victoria's spiritual counsel on a matter regarding his future. Colonel Blood was in an unhappy marriage and wanted to know if he should leave his wife.

Victoria and Colonel Blood were instantly drawn to each other. She said nothing about the attraction she felt for him but concentrated on the job he hired her to do. She passed into a trance, during which she announced unconsciously to herself that his future destiny was to be linked with hers in marriage. When Victoria came out of the trance, she told Blood what she saw.

Tennessee Claflin LIBRARY OF CONGRESS LC_USZ62134029

As both took such visions seriously, they pledged themselves to one another. "We were married by the powers in the air at that moment," Blood wrote in his memoirs.

Victoria and Blood began having an affair almost immediately after they met. Victoria believed a sexual relationship connected individuals not only physically but also spiritually. Much to the dismay of those who held to conventional standards that sex should be practiced only within the confines of marriage, Victoria openly expressed the joy derived from sexual encounters outside the institution. Her unconventional opinion brought criticism from so-called polite society and speculation that she engaged in prostitution. Colonel Blood was captivated by Victoria's unorthodox views. She abandoned her family and children and ran off with Blood to Dayton, Ohio. Blood divorced his wife and married Victoria on July 15, 1866.

After the wedding ceremony, the Bloods went to New York. Victoria held public healings and séances in New York City, and Blood joined her in her work.

When Victoria wasn't on stage, she was discussing her "free-love" theory with like-minded people who felt women should be able to voice their thoughts not only about whom they had sex with but also who should represent them in public office. Victoria's parents, siblings, and children followed her to New York. The Claflins were energized by the business opportunities available in New York. In December 1867 Victoria's spiritual "guardian" came to her in a dream and shared a prediction that promised to be beneficial to her and her family's future. According to the September 30, 1871, edition of the *Anglo-American Times*, the guardian wrote the message he wanted her to have on scroll. The document, which came to be known as "The Memorial of Victoria C. Woodhull," was a petition addressed to Congress. The document claimed under the Fourteenth Amendment the right of women as other "citizens of the United States" to vote in "the States wherein they reside." It noted that "the State of New York, of which she was a citizen, should be restrained by Federal authority from preventing her exercise of this constitutional right." When Victoria came out of her trance she took the scroll to her sister Tennessee and her father and told them what happened.

Buck believed the idea revealed to his daughter was controversial, and, given that it was delivered by a "spiritual guardian," he felt that taking the message to a curious audience would make money. Victoria and Tennessee were in favor of the venture, but they lacked capital to launch a new show and take the message of women's right to vote to the masses. Buck quickly found a financial supporter in Cornelius Vanderbilt. Vanderbilt, a seventy-three-year-old multimillionaire, frequently consulted spiritualists to communicate with his deceased parents and wife. In exchange for the funds to invest in the Woodhull and Claflin venture, Buck promised that his daughters would be his personal on-call spiritualists. Vanderbilt enthusiastically agreed.

Victoria's time with the wealthy man was spent predicting stock market trends. As one who claimed to see the future, she used her gift to advise him on what to buy and sell. Tennessee concentrated on laying hands on Vanderbilt to heal him of his arthritis and rheumatism.

Vanderbilt found the women bewitching. He grew quite fond of them and trusted them implicitly. He helped the sisters grow their own stock portfolio, and, with the financial freedom she realized from Vanderbilt's tutelage, Victoria began pursuing her goal to secure women's right to vote. Other women such as Elizabeth Cady Stanton and Harriet Beecher had the same objective in mind, but Victoria's preoccupation with spiritualism and following the directive of a guardian in the hereafter detracted from her credibility. As a result the most influential leaders in the movement kept their distance from her.

The stock market crash in 1869 did not adversely affect Victoria. Tennessee, Victoria, and Vanderbilt were some of the few who survived the ordeal. Not only did they arrive on the other side of the disaster with their fortunes intact, but they also made money in the process. Vanderbilt helped Victoria and Tennessee establish a brokerage firm in 1870. On February 5, 1870, the sisters became the first female Wall Street brokers. Wall Street veterans were shocked at the sight of women peddling stocks and were more than a little skeptical that they would be successful. According to an article in the March 9, 1964, edition of the *Oakland Tribune*, when word leaked to the market that Victoria and her sister's firm was backed by Vanderbilt, numerous investors entered their establishment. In three weeks the ladies reportedly coined $700,000.

The ladies' popularity grew as a result of their financial accomplishment. It also attracted the attention of law enforcement from jurisdictions where the women had prior trouble. When confronted by the police about the charges pending against them in Chicago and Pennsylvania, Tennessee claimed she wasn't the woman they wanted. The authorities didn't believe her. She was charged and bound over for trial. Both women lost their cases in court and were made to pay substantial fines.

Victoria worked hard to repair the damage the negative publicity caused their firm and her political ambitions. She persuaded civil rights leader Susan B. Anthony to write an article about the stockbrokerage firm operated by her and her sister, both now known as the "Queens of Finance." The article complimented the sisters' gift for making money but was not as generous in referring to their practice of spiritualism. Victoria wanted to be accepted by Anthony and her followers fighting to gain women's right to vote, but doubted she'd ever be able to fully secure their approval. She believed she had something to offer the cause and was compelled to make a difference.

In April 1870, Victoria Claflin Woodhull Blood declared herself a candidate for president of the United States. While mapping out her platform, she and her sister decided to branch out into another area of business. Using additional support provided by Vanderbilt, Victoria started a newspaper. It was called *Woodhull and Claflin's Weekly*. It began as a somewhat tame women's rights publication but wound up a tabloid-style periodical filled with sex and vice. The first issue of the paper was published on May 14, 1870, and the front page listed the reason for its existence. "This journal will be primarily devoted to the vital interests of people and will treat all matters freely and without reservation. It will support Victoria C. Woodhull for president with its whole strength. With one Victoria on the throne of England and another as president of the US there will be a sisterhood of Victorias," the confident, outspoken spiritualist wrote in one of the first editions of the newspaper.

While Victoria divided her time between campaigning for the highest office in the land and writing for *Woodhull and Claflin's Weekly*, Tennessee was working on other ways the paper could benefit herself and her sister. The sisters had schemed themselves into the upper strata of political leaders and lawmakers, and they had learned quickly they could blackmail those individuals by promising to keep their private lives out of the paper. Some believe it was because of such tactics that Victoria was granted the opportunity to speak before the House Judiciary Committee on women's suffrage at the National Women's Suffrage Association convention in January 1871.

The articles that appeared in *Woodhull and Claflin's Weekly* were just as contentious as Victoria's public addresses. The newspapers contained reports about corruption in local and national government, general gossip about some of the country's most elite, how-to divorce tips, directions on how to perform an abortion, how to operate a brothel, prostitution, and women's rights.

In February 1871, the sisters were sued for misappropriating money from their stockbroker clients. A court found the women guilty of embezzlement. Within a few weeks of the court's decision, Henry Beecher Stowe, minister and publisher of the newspaper the *Christian Union*, alleged that *Woodhull and Claflin's Weekly* was printing libel. Stowe offered no specifics, however. The court case and libel allegation devastated Victoria's personal life as well as her professional life. In early 1872, Victoria and Tennessee were forced to suspend publishing the newspaper for a short period of time.

Victoria tried to rise above the various setbacks and pressed forward with her run for the presidency. On May 10, 1872, she was the keynote speaker at the convention for her political party, the Equal Rights Party. She was officially nominated for president of the United States, and Frederick Douglass was listed as her running mate. *Woodhull and Claflin's Weekly* was up and running again after the nomination was made.

In retaliation for the negative attention she had received (primarily from the Beecher family), Victoria ran a story in September 1872 about an affair Henry Ward Beecher was having with a member of his congregation. In addition to the exposé about Stowe, the *Weekly* featured an article about a corrupt stockbroker named Luther Challis. According to information Tennessee offered to the paper, Challis frequently boasted about seducing young girls. He bragged that he would "ply them with alcohol first then have sex with them." The *Weekly* noted that Challis claimed "the bloody proof of the loss of one girl's virginity on his fingers." The scandalous issue of the newspaper was sent to many of the five thousand subscribers via the US Postal Service.

On November 2, 1872, an agent of the Society for the Suppression of Obscene Literature appeared before the US Commissioner and asked for the arrest of Victoria Woodhull and Tennessee Claflin. According to the November 7, 1872, edition of the Monticello, Iowa, newspaper the *Monticello Express,* the agent's request was promptly granted. "The sisters were arrested at their brokerage firm and driven to the United States marshal's office," the article noted. Victoria and Tennessee were subsequently charged with circulating obscene and indecent publications through the mail, the penalty for which, as prescribed by the statute, was imprisonment for one year and a fine of $500. Three thousand copies of the newspaper containing the alleged obscene matter were confiscated from the sisters' business.

The initial case against the sisters was eventually dismissed. From November 1872 to June 1873, Victoria and Tennessee were arrested seven additional times on similar obscenity and libel charges. They were acquitted each time they went to court. Paying for various attorneys to represent them led to bankruptcy and the collapse of *Woodhull and Claflin's Weekly*. Victoria's political party collapsed as well. Colonel Blood and Victoria divorced in 1878, and she remarried British banker John Biddulph Martin in 1883. The Martins moved to England shortly after they wed. Victoria died of old age at her home in North Park, England, on June 9, 1927. She was eighty-eight years old. Victoria's body was cremated, and her remains were scattered at sea.

Bibliography

General Sources

Adams, Ramon F., Natt N. Dodge, Wayne Gard, Dale Morgan, B. A. Botkin, Robert Easton, Oscar Lewis, Don Russell, and Oscar O. Winther. *The Book of the American West*. Simon & Schuster: New York, New York, 1963.

Alexander, Kent. *Legends of the Old West Trailblazers, Desperados, Wranglers, and Yarn-Spinners*. Friedman/Fairfax Publishers: New York, New York, 1994.

Ball, Eve. *In the Days of Victorio: Recollections of a Warm Springs Apache*. University of Arizona Press: Tucson, Arizona, 1970.

Beckwourth, James P., and Thomas D. Bonner (ed.). *The Life and Adventures of James P. Beckwourth*. University of Nebraska Press: Lincoln, Nebraska, 1981.

Burke, John. *The Legend of Baby Doe*. G.P. Putnam's Sons: New York, New York, 1974.

Calabro, Marian. *The Perilous Journey of the Donner Party*. Clarion Books: New York, New York, 1999.

Crum, Lola A., Jim Moran, Margaret Klenke, Russell Lupton, Daisy Plotner, Evelyn Steimel, Ann Warner, Veryle and Charles Wycoff, and Judith Young. *Dodge City and Ford County, Kansas 1870–1920 Pioneer Histories and Stories*. Ford County Historical Society: Dodge City, Kansas, 1996.

Crutchfield, James, Bill O'Neal, and Dale L. Walker. *Legends of the Wild West*. Publications International, Ltd.: Lincolnwood, Illinois, 1995.

Gabriel, Mary. *Notorious Victoria: The Life of Victoria Woodhull, Uncensored*. Algonquin Books: Chapel Hill, North Carolina, 1998.

Grant, Matthew G. *Elizabeth Blackwell Pioneer Doctor*. Publications Associations Illustrated: Chicago, Illinois, 1974.

Hassrick, Royal B. *The Colorful Story of the American West*. Octopus Books Limited: London, England, 1975.

Lardner, W. B., and M. J. Brock. *History of Placer and Nevada Counties California*. Historic Records Company: Los Angeles, California, 1924.

Largo, Michael. *The Portable Obituary: How the Famous, Rich, and Powerful Really Died*. Harper Collins: New York, New York, 2007.

Luchetti, Cathy. *Medicine Women: The Story of Early-American Women Doctors*. Crown Publishing: New York, New York, 1998.

Lucia, Ellis. *Klondike Kate 1873–1957*. Comstock Editions, Inc.: Sausalito, California, 1962.

May, Robin. *The Story of the Wild West*. The Hamlyn Publishing Group: New York, New York, 1978.

McGlashan, C.F. *History of the Donner Party: A Tragedy of the Sierra*. Stanford University Press: Stanford, California, 1940.

Miller, Floyd. *Bill Tilghman: Marshal of the Last Frontier*. Doubleday & Company, Inc.: Garden City, New York, 1968.

Miller, Nyle H., and Joseph W. Snell. *Great Gunfighters of the Kansas Cowtowns 1867–1886*. University of Nebraska Press: Lincoln, Nebraska, 1963.

Nash, Jay Robert. *Encyclopedia of Western Lawmen & Outlaws*. Paragon House: New York, New York, 1989.

Rittenhouse, Mignon. *The Amazing Nellie Bly*. E.P. Dutton & Company, Inc.: New York, New York, 1956.

Sargent, Shirley. *Pioneers in Petticoats: Yosemite's Early Women 1856–1900*. Trans-Anglo Books: Los Angeles, California, 1966.

Segale, Sister Blandina. *At the End of the Santa Fe Trail*. The Bruce Publishing Company: Milwaukee, Wisconsin, 1948.

Utley, Robert. *Encyclopedia of the American West*. Random House: New York, New York, 1977.

Woods, Lawrence. *Asa Shinn Mercer: Western Promoter and Newspaperman 1839–1917*. The Arthur Clark Company: Spokane, Washington, 2003.

Zebelle-Derounian-Stodola, Katheryn, and James Arthur Levernie. *The Indian Captivity Narrative 1500–1900*. Penguin Classics: New York, New York, 1998.

Newspapers

Atlantic Evening News, Atlantic, Iowa, April 1, 1908.

Billings Gazette, Billings, Montana, October 11, 1919.

Blockton News, Blockton, Iowa, September 5, 1929.

Boston Post, Boston, Massachusetts, January 28, 1922.

The Cedar Rapids Evening Gazette, Cedar Rapids, Iowa, August 21, 1895, and March 17, 1903.

The Clinton Herald, Clinton, Iowa, June 6, 1922.

Columbus Daily Herald, Columbus, Ohio, August 19, 1895.

The Daily Ardmoreite, Ardmore, Oklahoma, January 2, 1908, and July 18, 1932.

Decatur Herald, Decatur, Illinois, January 23, 1929.

Defiance Democrat, Defiance County, Ohio, February 20, 1864.

Des Moines Register, Des Moines, Iowa, October 26, 1964.

Essex County Republican, Keesville, New York, May 7, 1943.

The Fort Wayne Journal-Gazette, Fort Wayne, Indiana, October 1, 1919.

The Fort Wayne Sentinel, Fort Wayne, Indiana, June 1, 1910.

The Herald, Fall River, Massachusetts, March 20, 1903.

The Hutchinson News, Hutchinson, Kansas, August 9, 1912; August 12, 1912; and November 4, 1924.

Indianapolis Daily Journal, Indianapolis, Indiana, January 22, 1864, and February 12, 1864.

The Kansas City Star, Kansas City, Missouri, September 28, 1919, and November 2, 1924.

Kokomo Tribune, Kokomo, Indiana, May 12, 1977 and February 11, 2002.

Lethbridge Herald, Lethbridge, Alberta, February 22, 1957.

Lowell Sun, Lowell, Massachusetts, October 9, 1949.

Manitowoc Daily Herald, Manitowoc, Wisconsin, December 29, 1902.

Mason City Globe-Gazette, Mason City, Iowa, August 22, 1938.

Muskogee Phoenix, Muskogee, Oklahoma, January 15, 1910.

New Castle News, New Castle, Pennsylvania, June 6, 1910, and March 12, 1935.

The News-Palladium, Benton Harbor, Michigan, August 2, 1961.

The New York Times, New York, New York, September 30, 1865; January 26, 1911; and October 21, 1964.

Oakland Tribune, Oakland, California, October 20, 1910; July 22, 1911; July 25, 1911; January 22, 1929; March 8, 1935; June 21, 1942; and December 22, 1977.

The Odessa American, Odessa, Texas, June 30, 1968.

The Pella Chronicle, Pella, Iowa, April 13, 1922.

Reno Gazette, Reno, Nevada, July 17, 1928.

The Salt Lake Tribune, Salt Lake, Utah, April 26, 1943.

San Antonio Light, San Antonio, Texas, February 16, 1930.

The Sandusky Star-Journal, Sandusky, Ohio, September 23, 1919.

Scandia Journal, Scandia, Kansas, April 15, 1904.

Sullivan Democrat, Sullivan County, New York, January 22, 1903.

The Syracuse Herald, Syracuse, New York, March 15, 1908.

The Washington Post, Washington, D.C., July 24, 1908.

Waterloo Daily Tribune, Waterloo, Iowa, October 20, 1964.

Wichita Daily Times, Wichita, Kansas, June 4, 1936.

Magazine

"Western Legends," *Golden West Magazine*, May 1968, Vol. 4, No. 4.

Websites

www.ancestry.com. Sarah Ann Newton Horn. Accessed September 3, 2014.

http://carrcentral.org/Family%20stories.htm. Chalk Beeson. Accessed January 15, 2015.

http://www.historynet.com/california-gold-rush. Baby Doe Tabor. Accessed January 20, 2015.

www.imdb.com. Accessed January 15, 2015.

www.tshaonline.org/handbook/online/articles. John Simpson Chisum. Accessed January 28, 2014.

www.tshaonline.org/handbook/online/articles. Sarah Ann Newton Horn. Accessed September 3, 2014.

http://www.mommd.com/lookingback.shtml. Elizabeth Blackwell. Accessed January 15, 2015.

http://www.nellieblyonline.com. Nellie Bly. Accessed January 15, 2015.

About the Author

Chris Enss is a *New York Times* best-selling author who has been writing about characters of the Old West for more than a dozen years. She has penned more than thirty published books on the subject. Her book *Object: Matrimony: The Risky Business of Mail-Order Matchmaking on the Western Frontier* (Globe Pequot) won the Elmer Kelton Award for best nonfiction book of 2013. Another recent Enss title, *Sam Sixkiller: Cherokee Frontier Lawman* (also Globe Pequot), was named Outstanding Book on Oklahoma History by the Oklahoma Historical Society. Enss also has received the Spirit of the West Alive award, cosponsored by the *Wild West Gazette*, celebrating her efforts to keep the spirit of the Old West alive for future generations.